W9-AGA-575

BEST OF

Shanghai

Damian Harper

How to use this book

Colour-Coding & Maps

Each chapter has a colour code along the banner at the top of the page which is also used for text and symbols on maps (eg all venues reviewed in the Highlights chapter are orange on the maps). The fold-out maps inside the front and back covers are numbered from 1 to 8. All sights and venues in the text have map references; eg (4, B1) means Map 4, grid reference B1. See p96 for map symbols.

Prices

Multiple prices listed with reviews (eg Y10/5) usually indicate adult/child admission to a venue. Meal cost and room rate categories are listed at the start of the Eating and Sleeping chapters, respectively.

Text Symbols

☎ telephone
✉ address
🖳 email/website address
$ admission
☾ opening hours
ⓘ information
Ⓜ metro
🚍 bus
⚓ ferry/boat
🚆 train
♿ wheelchair access
✕ on site/nearby eatery
☻ child-friendly venue

Best of Shanghai
1st edition – January 2006

Published by Lonely Planet Publications Pty Ltd
ABN 36 005 607 983

Australia Head Office, Locked Bag 1, Footscray, Vic 3011
☎ 03 8379 8000 fax 03 8379 8111
🖳 talk2us@lonelyplanet.com.au
USA 150 Linden St, Oakland, CA 94607
☎ 510 893 8555 toll free 800 275 8555
fax 510 893 8572
🖳 info@lonelyplanet.com
UK 72–82 Rosebery Avenue, London EC1R 4RW
☎ 020 7841 9000 fax 020 7841 9001
🖳 go@lonelyplanet.co.uk

This title was commissioned in Lonely Planet's Melbourne office and produced by: **Commissioning Editor** Rebecca Chau **Coordinating Editor** Trent Holden **Coordinating Cartographer** Andrew Smith **Layout Designer** David Kemp **Proofer** Margedd Heliosz **Indexer** Trent Holden **Cartographer** Jolyon Philcox **Managing Cartographer** Corinne Waddell **Cover Designer** Rebecca Dandens **Project Manager** Chris Love **Mapping Development** Paul Piaia **Desktop Publishing Support** Mark Germanchis **Thanks to** Carol Chandler, Celia Wood, Darren O'Connell, Jane Thompson, Rebecca Lalor, Sally Darmody, Adriana Mammarella.

Photographs by Lonely Planet Images and Greg Elms except for the following: p7, p9, p10, p17, p18, p19, p22, p23, p32, p34, p36, p42, p44, p45, p46, p47, p51, p53, p54, p55, p59, p67, p68, p71, p72, p74, p78, p81 Phil Weymouth; p13, p27, p76 Bradley Mayhew; p37 Diana Mayfield; p38 Juliet Coombe; p39 Bruce Yuan-Yue Bi; p65 Dallas Stribley. **Cover photograph** Group of people practising Tai Chi at dawn along the Bund, Shanghai, Keren Su/Getty Images. All images are copyright of the photographers unless otherwise indicated. Many of the images in this guide are available for licensing from Lonely Planet Images: www.lonelyplanetimages.com.

ISBN 1 74059 497 5

Printed through Colorcraft Ltd, Hong Kong.
Printed in China

Contents

From the Publisher

AUTHOR
Damian Harper

Born in London and educated at Winchester College, Damian abandoned a directionless career in bookselling to study Modern and Classical Chinese at London's School of Oriental and African Studies. His degree took him to Beijing, which deepened his affection for the country. Damian hightailed it to Hong Kong for a year upon graduation, before chancing upon a new life as a freelance writer. To date, he has contributed to 10 Lonely Planet books and is currently living long-term on the borders of the French Concession in Shanghai with his Qingdao-born wife, Dai Min, his son, Timothy Benjamin (Jiafu) and daughter, Emma Rosalind (Jiale).

Special thanks to my wife for her unflagging patience and to my children for being who they are. Gratitude also to the editorial and cartographic staff at Lonely Planet for seeing this book through from conception to publication. Last but not least, much appreciation to all who offered suggestions and advice along the way.

LONELY PLANET AUTHORS
Why is our travel information the best in the world? It's simple: our authors are independent, dedicated travellers. They don't research using just the Internet or phone, and they don't take freebies in exchange for positive coverage. They travel widely, to all the popular spots and off the beaten track. They personally visit thousands of hotels, restaurants, cafés, bars, galleries, palaces, museums and more – and they take pride in getting all the details right, and telling it how it is. For more, see the authors section on **www.lonelyplanet.com**.

PHOTOGRAPHER
Greg Elms

Having been a contributor to Lonely Planet for over 15 years, Greg Elms has completed numerous commissions in that time. The Best Of and City guides in particular provide a chaotic mix of search-and-shoot photography in often less than ideal conditions. In Shanghai he needed to consume literally litres of sports drinks in the oppressive August heat while racing between shots and negotiating Shanghai's frenetic streets.

Greg's interest in photography began during a stint of winery work in South Australia's Barossa Valley, where regular consumption of the local wines forced him to lie on his back and gaze skyward at the spectacular cloudscapes of streaking cirrus that formed in the jet stream above the Valley. Greg began his commercial career by completing a three year Bachelor of Arts in Photography at Royal Melbourne Institute of Technology, then assisting a photographer for two years before taking off on a travel odyssey around Australia, Southeast Asia, India, East Africa, Egypt, Israel and Europe. Eventually settling down to a freelance career in Melbourne, he now works regularly for magazines, graphic designers, advertising agencies and of course book publishers such as Lonely Planet.

SEND US YOUR FEEDBACK
We love to hear from travellers – your comments keep us on our toes and help make our books better. Our well-travelled team reads every word on what you loved or loathed about this book. Although we cannot reply individually to postal submissions, we always guarantee that your feedback goes straight to the appropriate authors, in time for the next edition – and the most useful submissions are rewarded with a free book. To send us your updates – and find out about Lonely Planet events, newsletters and travel news – visit our award-winning website: **www.lonelyplanet.com/feedback**.

Note: We may edit, reproduce and incorporate your comments in Lonely Planet products such as guidebooks, websites and digital products, so let us know if you don't want your comments reproduced or your name acknowledged. For a copy of our privacy policy visit **www.lonelyplanet.com/privacy**.

Introducing Shanghai

Typifying a stylish new China and a riveting success story still in the telling, Shanghai is the Chinese city foreigners are raring to see. Its invigorating cocktail of energy and excess is what the new People's Republic is all about, and in today's global village, Shanghai is the talk of the town.

From piping-hot *xiǎolóngbāo* (steamed dumplings) to fusion cuisine, charming 1930s-style European cottages and traditional *shíkùmén* households to sleek skyscrapers, Shanghai is where old and new China most extravagantly overlap. Like Hong Kong before it, Shanghai is also a fascinating entrée to the China experience: Western enough to raise an eyebrow, but Chinese enough to turn heads and stop you in your tracks.

Brashly modern in parts, but at heart a traditional community, Shanghai's version of the future is hardly textbook. The Shanghainese won't think twice about shopping in pyjamas, or ballroom dancing in the park, and there are few cities where you can hear the growl of an Aston Martin over a cavalcade of bicycle bells. Locals may grumble there are too many people – and there are – but it's these density levels that give Shanghai its dawn-to-dusk buzz.

Chinese history being what it is, their revolutionary zeal is a closed book, but the energetic Shanghainese – regarded by the rest of China as shrewd, savvy albeit stingy – have cobbled together one of the world's leading cities. Only 160 or so years in the making, this idiosyncratic metropolis has arrived at a marvellous bedlam of stylish bars, chic restaurants, imposing architecture, tranquil temples, magnificent museum collections, hectic markets and sophisticated shopping malls.

Pudong's dazzling skyline is surely China's most audacious display of wherewithal, but you only have to wander the Bund and the tree-lined streetscapes of the French Concession to find the style and poise that first put the city on the world map. Enjoy your visit!

The spectre of the past still haunts Shanghai's streets, the Bund

Neighbourhoods

Shanghai's mighty tangle of roads and absence of a clear-cut centre of gravity can make for rapid disorientation. Helpfully, the **Huangpu River** splices the city into two distinct entities: **Puxi** (west of the river) and **Pudong** (east of the river). Most travellers gravitate toward Shanghai's stylish and charming districts west of the river, while launching occasional forays into Pudong, which only impinges on the consciousness for its top-league hotels, racy architecture and museums.

Without Beijing's dynastic feng shui–ridden design, central Shanghai's plan draws instead from its foreign concession layout and post-1990 Pudong boom-era conception. The original heart of old Chinese Shanghai – the **Old Town** – today lies off-centre and south of that world-famous monument to the good old bad old days – **the Bund** – the easternmost and paramount point of interest in Puxi. Unfolding in a splash of nocturnal neon west from the Bund, **East Nanjing Rd**, Shanghai's most famous shopping street, ushers pedestrians to **Renmin Square** and its landmark sights. Barely pausing for breath, **West Nanjing Rd** slices on through the business district and the expat residential stronghold of **Jing'an**, studded with shopping malls and bars.

The city's other main commercial drag – stylish **Huaihai Rd** – cuts through the heart of the old **French Concession**, a delightful district occupying a huge area west of the Old Town and decorated with charming tree-lined streets and 1930s villa architecture. In the east of the French Concession, **Xintiandi** musters a stylish blend of modern restaurants, bars and old Shanghai *shíkùmén* housing.

The old Jesuit mission was located in south Shanghai's traffic-clogged **Xujiahui** district, its ecclesiastical remains now overshadowed by a confluence of huge shopping malls and towers. Few short-stay visitors make it to **Hongqiao** or the modern expat ghetto of **Gubei** in the west of Shanghai, marked by hotels, supermarkets, hypermarkets and iffy transport links.

Those treading the Jewish trail will sooner or later find themselves in **Hongkou** district north of Suzhou creek, the traditional heart of Shanghai's Jewish community.

OFF THE BEATEN TRACK

One of the world's most populous and least laid-back cities, Shanghai's hard-working, can-do mentality has sent peace and solitude packing. But unexpected languorous pockets can still be eked out from the surging streets. Evade the honking black VW Santanas and get a breather at the Bonomi Café in the Hengshan Moller Villa (left), or take a pew in the cool silence of St Ignatius Cathedral or the Catholic Church in Qibao. Last but not least, flee the skyscrapers at Gongqing Park.

Itineraries

If time is tight and you need to rapidly bring Shanghai to heel, these itineraries will help you squeeze the best out of the city in the shortest time. The top sights are here, with a sprinkling of less well-known diversions.

Day One

Be an early bird and catch the exercise enthusiasts on the Bund, before plunging into the commercial maelstrom of Nanjing Rd en route to Renmin Square and the Shanghai Museum. Then dive into the Renmin Park metro, shuttle across to Pudong, breeze through the Shanghai Municipal History Museum as an appetiser to sizing up the modern city below from the 88th floor of the Jinmao Tower.

SHANGHAI LOWS
- Crossing the road (see p34)
- Finding a taxi with a rear seat belt
- The grim no-man's-land of the Pudong bar scene
- Pricey ticket gouging at the Oriental Pearl TV Tower
- Extortionate restaurant wine lists
- The way checkout girls drop your change on the counter instead of into your hand
- The metro rush hour
- Noxious air quality
- Shanghai's public sculpture

Day Two

Be first in line at the Yuyuan Gardens and load up later on *xiǎolóngbāo* (steamed dumplings) at the nearby Nanxiang Steamed Bun Restaurant. Spend the afternoon walking it all off wandering the French Concession, navigating Xintiandi and grappling with Xiangyang Market, before concluding the day on a civilised note at one of the district's stylish restaurants, bars or live music venues.

Day Three

Bookmark the morning for exploring the Jade Buddha Temple before hopping on the metro from Shanghai Train Station to Xujiahui for its Jesuit artifacts and dining options. Reboard the metro to Middle Henan Rd station or Lujiazui and enjoy a panoramic Huangpu River cruise. Back on dry land, try to fit in a joint-twisting acrobatics show in the early evening.

The future is upon us, bird's eye view from Oriental Pearl TV Tower

Highlights

THE BUND 外滩 (5, J4)

Shanghai's most august row of grand buildings parades itself on the Bund (waitan), its doddery and gaunt haughtiness scowling at the newfangled glass and steel Pudong horizon beyond. Nowhere else in Shanghai are the retiring symbols of Western hegemony so deftly contrasted with the signs of growing Chinese clout.

INFORMATION

- ⊠ First East Zhongshan Rd
- Ⓜ Middle Henan Rd
- ⓧ Jean Georges (p49), M on the Bund (p49), Number 5 (p49), Whampoa Club (p50)
- ⓖ poor

Originally a muddy towpath, the name Bund is an Anglo-Indian word for an embankment, and it was to this once grubby riverside perch that the foreign banks and trading houses brought their plutocratic vision. The buildings badly need a sand-blasting to scour away the generations of bus fumes, but this remains Shanghai's most impressive slice of history. For a rundown of the **HSBC Building**, the **Peace Hotel**, the **Customs House** and other notable buildings along the Bund, see the Sights & Activities chapter (p20) and the Bund Walk (p33). Cutting through curtains of fumes and ozone, views of **Pudong** unveil a brash skyline of (hit-and-miss) architecture, built upon bold aspirations and galloping GDP growth.

Amble along the elevated riverside promenade alongside the Huangpu River for an energetic carnival of kiosks, hawkers flogging toys and gadgets, kites soaring overhead, the endless screech of 'Huānyíng guānglín' ('Welcome'), photographers, coin-operated telescopes and all the mayhem of China's tourism boom. You can even weigh yourself or get your blood pressure checked. Boat journeys along the **Huangpu River** afford first-rate panoramas of the Bund chugging in and out of view. For a more sedate and dignified appreciation of the local charms, dine at **M on the Bund**, where a night-time or twilight visit allows the setting to fully work its magic.

DON'T MISS

- A coffee on the 2nd floor Bonomi Café (p52) in the HSBC Building
- A wander through the lobby of the Peace Hotel (p21)
- Waibaidu (Garden) Bridge, the Pujiang Hotel and the Russian Consulate

SHANGHAI MUSEUM 上海博物馆 (5, F5)

A circular building (designed to replicate a *dǐng* – an ancient Chinese bronze vessel) at the eye of the city, China's premier museum combines a spectacular collection with a first-rate museum layout design within. Compared with China's stale and under-funded provincial museum world, the Shanghai Museum is on another planet. Excellent lighting, clear captions in English, escalators, light-filled atrium and well spaced-out exhibits conspire to effortlessly guide visitors past a delicious collection. The only grit in the ointment is the poor air circulation. Those who can tell their underglaze blue moon flasks from their *dòucǎi ewers*, will find the **Ancient Chinese Ceramics Gallery** gorgeous for its chubby-faced Tang dynasty female figures, cool celadon bowls, spotless

> **DON'T MISS**
> • Celadon Vase with ancient bronze design, Zande Lou Gallery (Ancient Chinese Ceramics Gallery)
> • Ming dynasty *déhuà* statues of Guanyin, the Goddess of Mercy, Zande Lou Gallery (Ancient Chinese Ceramics Gallery)
> • Western Zhou three-legged *dǐng*, Ancient Chinese Bronzes Gallery

The world's biggest dumpling steamer?

Qinghua (blue-and-white) porcelain, elegant *déhuà* (blanc-de-chine: white glazed porcelain) effigies, playful *dòucǎi* pieces and elaborate famille-rose (*fěncǎi*) ceramics. Equally magnificent are the patina greens of the **Ancient Chinese Bronzes Gallery**, with its impressive three-legged *dǐng*, *zūn* (bowls) and *jué* (wine pourers), many patterned with fierce-looking animistic *tāotiè* (a mythical beast) designs.

The **Chinese Painting Gallery** guides visitors past works from the Tang, Song, Yuan and Ming dynasties and furniture enthusiasts will be delighted by the carved rosewood and sandalwood pieces in the **Ming and Qing Furniture Gallery**, including a large canopy bed and delightful chairs from the Ming dynasty.

The **Calligraphy Gallery** can only be fully appreciated by expert readers of Chinese, but delve into the culture, art and clothing of China's colourful patchwork of non-Han Chinese ethnic minorities (p25) at the **Minority Nationalities Art Gallery**. Other galleries include the **Ancient Chinese Jade Gallery**, the **Coin Gallery**, the **Seal Gallery** and the **Ancient Chinese Sculpture Gallery**. The ground floor **museum shop** has some excellent books and the 2nd-floor tea house is at hand when lethargy inevitably hits. Visitors with a special interest in the arts of China will find one visit insufficient (p27).

INFORMATION

☎ 6372 3500
🖳 www.shanghaimuseum.net
✉ 201 Renmin Ave
$ Y20/5; audio tour Y40
🕙 9am-5pm (last entry 4pm)
Ⓜ Renmin Square/Renmin Park
♿ OK
🍴 2nd-floor tea house

YUYUAN GARDENS 豫园 (4, B1)

Comparable to the classical Chinese gardens of Suzhou (p37), the 2-hectare Yuyuan Gardens are famed for their tranquilising harmonies of light and shade and rock and water. Crowds shatter the equilibrium, however, and the sedative effect of this picturesque pocket really all depends on how fast the turnstiles are spinning.

The gardens were founded by the Pan family, rich Ming dynasty officials. The gardens took 18 years (1559–77) to be nurtured to fruition, only to be ransacked during both the Opium War and the Taiping Rebellion. Today, the restored gardens are a fine example of Ming garden design.

Enjoy a cuppa at Yuyuan Gardens tea house

The whole composition is a picturesque exercise in equilibrium, with corridors, rockeries, pools, bridges and pavilions providing the aesthetic balance. The rockeries, resembling outsized pumice stones (often inexpertly welded together with cement), appear wan and washed-out. The gardens are small, but they are magnified by an ingenious use of rocks and alcoves that create pockets of space. The dragon is a common motif here and is present in over 300 examples. Highlights of the gardens include the **Three Ears of Corn Hall**, the first pavilion facing you as you enter (where a map of the garden layout can be found), the **Exquisite Jade Rock** and the **Hall of Heralding Spring**, which was where the Small Swords Society convened prior to their uprising. Also look out for the gilded woodwork of the **Ancient Stage**, first built in 1888.

It's well worth coming here in spring to catch the magnolias in bloom. Early birds catch the worm, while later arrivals get costume hire and foraging Japanese tour groups, and weekends are strictly for those who like their tourists wall-to-wall. The entrance to the gardens is next to the famous Mid-Lake Pavilion Teahouse, linked to the edges of the pool by a zigzag bridge, designed by feng shui necromancers to steer bad spirits off course.

The gardens are attached to a lively bazaar, with every square inch occupied by restaurants and souvenir shops, apart from the sacred territory that's occupied by the Temple of the Town Gods. The sprawl of antique sellers continues with gusto down Central Fangbang Rd.

INFORMATION

☎ 6373 7522
✉ 218 Anren St
$ Y30/10
🕑 8.30am-5.30pm; last tickets sold 5pm
Ⓜ Middle Henan Rd
♿ poor

PUDONG 浦东 (6)

A brave new world of rocketing high-rise towers and five star hotels has abruptly unfolded in Pudong, Shanghai's most ostentatious display of its can-do mentality and a showcase for China's growing ego.

On the east side of the Huangpu River, Pudong is unlike other parts of China: there's zero Soviet-era architecture, no historic temples, the public loos are clean and the world's first (and last?) Maglev train (p26) warps at over Mach 0.3 through what was – just 15 years ago – mere farmland. The rush into real estate has embedded some artless architecture in the Pudong skyline and the overall conception has neither charm nor soul, but sporadic successes – the crystalline beauty of the Jinmao Tower for example – reward exploration.

INFORMATION

Ⓜ Lujiazui, Dongchang Rd, Dongfang Rd, Shanghai Science & Technology Museum, Century Park
✖ Danieli's (p56)
♿ good

From the perspective of the Bund at least, Pudong's signature image is the love-it-or-loathe-it 468m-tall **Oriental Pearl TV Tower**, its baubles and reach-for-the-sky rocket lines suggesting a monument to the 1950s atom age. The tower lacks oomph, but the views from the top spheroid are astronomic. Beneath the tower is the fantastic **Shanghai Municipal History Museum**, a first-rate tour through the history of the city, and reason alone to be in Pudong.

The nearby **Shanghai Natural Wild Insect Kingdom** and **Shanghai Aquarium** are both attractions for kids.

The lofty perch of the Grand Hyatt, the **Jinmao Tower** is a true jaw dropper. Take the high-speed lift to the observation deck on the 88th floor to see if you can make out the earth's curvature, or sink a high-altitude drink at Cloud 9.

At the end of Century Blvd, the **Shanghai Science & Technology Museum** has a dazzling display, aimed at tykes and young boffins.

Love is in the air at M on the Bund, overlooking Pudong's glitzy skyline

SHANGHAI ZOO 上海动物园 (2, A2)

With its well-groomed menagerie of beasts, this huge zoo is not only one of Shanghai's fun attractions, it's also one of the city's most picturesque and spacious expanses of green. The animals – from woolly twin-humped Bactrian Camels to spindly legged giraffes – are definitely crowd pleasers but Shanghai folk are also here to take advantage of the wide-open lawns for a spot of picnic. Clean and well-tended

INFORMATION

☎ 6268 7775
✉ 2381 Hongqiao Rd
💲 Y30; elephant show Y20
🕐 5am-6pm 1 Apr-30 June,
   5am-7pm 1 July-30 Sept,
   6am-6pm 1 Oct-31 Mar
🚌 No 831, 48, 328
♿ OK

shaded paths thread through old-growth trees (cherry plums, camphor, *osmanthus*, silk trees, pines, pomegranate and others) and dense foliage, while honking **tour buggies** (Y10; depart every 10 to 15 minutes, 8.30am to 4.30pm) whisk visitors about. Rotate to the top of the creaking **big wheel** (Y5) for long views over the zoo. The little ones can get in free to the **Children's Zoo** where they can shower chubby piglets and billy goats with handfuls of grain, prance about on the bouncing castle (Y10), fish for goldfish (Y2 per minute) or ride ponies (Y5). The lake at the heart of the zoo is delightfully ringed by willows, bamboo and pines. Several outfits in the zoo offer over-priced snacks (Taiwan sausages Y3; corn on the cob Y4) and drinks along the route, so stock up beforehand for when you get the munchies or need to slake a thirst. Maps (Y1) are available from the information kiosk at the entrance. You can pass on the patience-testing elephant show if you want, although children will adore handing out sticks of sugar cane to be scooped up by the inquisitive trunks.

SHANGHAI-RISE

Until the 1980s, the 83.8m-tall brick Park Hotel (1934) was the tallest building in town. The Jinmao Tower of its day, the Chinese said that if you looked all the way to its roof, your hat would fall off. The city has railroaded through some ugly architecture, but gems still sparkle on the skyline. Resembling one of Dr Octopus' mechanical claws, Tomorrow Square (left) ambitiously reaches for the stratosphere over Puxi. Work has finally begun on the World Financial Centre, destined to be the world's tallest building when completed in 2007. Still a hole in the ground at the time of writing, the stop-start project dates back to 1997.

JADE BUDDHA TEMPLE 玉佛寺 (5, A3)

While it's a gala tourist festival and the tinkle of the tourist dollar jars with the sacred chanting of monks and birds chirping in the temple's *Magnolia grandiflora,* it nevertheless remains one of Shanghai's most important Buddhist shrines. Festooned with red lanterns, the halls and courtyards of the saffron-coloured Jade Buddha Temple glitter with fine effigies and temple ornaments, but the highlight is its namesake 1.9m tall **Jade Buddha** *(yùfó).* Displayed in a carved wood cabinet, the pale-green, cool effigy of Sakyamuni – from Myanmar (Burma) – is sadly unapproachable, but you can gaze at it from the other side of a wooden barrier. At the foot of the stairs

Statue of Buddha, Jade Buddha Temple.

leading up to the jade statue, a large full-form character is penned in black ink on a scroll; the character is '*chén*' (dust), a Buddhist metaphor for this human world. Also worth investigation is the similarly styled **Reclining Buddha** *(wòfó),* amid pieces for sale in the 'religious article shop'. The smiling white jade figure, head propped up on one palm and other arm lying femininely on his side, represents Sakyamuni on the point of death before entering nirvana. Opposite is a much larger and less artful modern copy in stone. Other marvellous features of the temple include the extravagant statue of **Weituo** in the **Hall of Heavenly Kings**, displayed back-to-back with **Milefo** in a fabulous case with glass panes.

The main hall – the **Great Treasure Hall** – is dedicated to the worship of the past, present and future buddhas, flanked by towering gilded **Luohan** *(arhat)* and supported by a figure of **Guanyin** at the rear, standing atop an alligator's head. The temple has a popular 100% **vegetarian restaurant** attached. A good time to visit the temple is on the occasion of the Chinese New Year.

INFORMATION

☎ 6266 3668

✉ 170 Anyuan Rd

$ Y10 (Y10 extra to see the Jade Buddha)

🕑 8am-4.30pm

Ⓜ Shanghai Railway Station (taxi Y10 from here)

Ⓥ vegetarian restaurant

♿ poor

LONGHUA TEMPLE & PAGODA 龙华寺与龙华塔 (2, B3)

The saffron-coloured halls of this historic temple constitute Shanghai's oldest, most extensive and best-preserved temple complex, where the constant band of worshippers and thick fug of incense generates a palpable sense of reverence. Inside the first hall sits a corpulent statue of **Milefo**, the Laughing Buddha (see p23) and a representation of Maitreya. Flanking the next courtyard are the triple-eaved **drum and bell towers**; the right-hand hall also serves as a shrine to **Dizang Wang**, Buddhist God of the Underworld. Interestingly, the next hall to the north is the **Hall of Heavenly Kings**, usually the first hall in Buddhist temples. The first statue facing you as you enter is a notable statue of the **Maitreya Buddha**, here cross-legged, wearing a crown and more divinely natured compared to his more popular representation. Disconcertingly large statues of the **Four Heavenly Kings** rise up on either side. Seated in neat rows within the **Luohan Hall** is a glittering constellation of 1000 **Luohan** (*arhat*) and the main hall – the **Great Treasure Hall** – encloses a large effigy of Sakyamuni seated on a lotus flower. At the rear of the hall rises a copper-coloured, wooden statue of **Guanyin**, facing north. Beyond the main hall is a vegetarian restaurant and a further imposing hall – the **Sanshengbao Hall** – with a golden trinity of Buddhist statues. In front of the temple entrance rises the (sadly off-limits) seven-storey **Longhua Pagoda**, originally erected in AD 977. The best time to visit the temple is during the Longhua Temple Fair, held on the third day of the third month of the lunar calendar. A short walk west along Longhua Rd is the **Longhua Flower and Bird Market**, a relaxing stretch of chirping crickets and bird song.

INFORMATION

☎ 6457 6327
✉ 2853 Longhua Rd
$ Y10
☺ 7am-5pm
Ⓜ Xujiahui, then bus No 44

PAGODA CONSTRUCTION

Towering above Chinese temples, the Chinese pagoda *(tǎ)* typically served as a library for Buddhist sutras, and frequently as a reliquary for sacred Buddhist objects, which were stored underground. Wooden pagodas and their sacred texts often went up in sheets of flame and others were levelled during war and revolt. The same fate befell many Chinese temples, and pagodas – devoid of their temples – are a common sight across China. Only a few pagodas ornament Shanghai, but both Suzhou (p37) and Hangzhou (p38) have some fine examples.

BIBLIOTHECA ZI-KA-WEI & ST IGNATIUS CATHEDRAL
徐家汇藏书楼, 天主教堂 (8, B2)

Among the Jesuit monuments littering Xujiahui in south Shanghai is the imposing St Ignatius Catholic Library, the **Bibliotheca Zi-Ka-Wei**, established in 1847 by the local Jesuit mission. Home to over 560,000 volumes in Greek, Latin and other languages, the library is housed in a splendid old building with verandas and shutters. You can enter the reading room upstairs with its fabulous ceiling and collection of old books on China in English or take the 15-minute tour of the library itself and its magnificent collection on Saturdays. Taking up residence on the ground floor, the well-lit and spacious **Wan Fung Art Gallery** is a further zone of period features, polished floor boards, some spectacular paintings, local sculpture and prints. North of the library rises the cruciform-shaped **St Ignatius Cathedral**, a twin-spired red-brick church with two belfries and a statue of Christ above the door, flanked by the four apostles. A long span of gothic arches, its nave is ornamented on the outside with menacing gargoyles. Much of the church's stained glass is sadly missing, but note how the ecclesiastical architecture of the church is echoed in surrounding buildings. Over the roaring traffic on the other side of North Caoxi Rd stands a further Jesuit monument, the former **St Ignatius Convent**, now the **Ye Olde Station Restaurant**, a fine place for Shanghai cuisine and a taste of the city in the old days.

INFORMATION
☎ 6487 4095 ext 208
✉ 80 North Caoxi Rd
☉ 1-4.30pm Sat & Sun; library tours 1-4pm Sat
Ⓜ Xujiahui
✗ Ye Olde Station Restaurant (p58)

ZIKAWEI
Missionaries from the Society of Jesus (the Jesuits) first arrived in Shanghai in 1842, soon after the first European arrivals. As their influence grew, Xujiahui (pronounced Zikawei in the Shanghai dialect) – a village five miles southwest of town – was selected as the centre of their mission. First built in 1847, the Zikawei Library contained 200,000 volumes (with 80,000 in European languages) at its peak. The mission was discontinued after the Communist victory but some of its ecclesiastical architecture survives. Historical photographs of Xujiahui in its heyday can be seen at the Bibliotheca Zi-Ka-Wei (above).

Celebrating a new purchase at Wan Fung Art Gallery, Xujiahui

FRENCH CONCESSION 法国租界 (3)

Shanghai's hippest bars and swishiest restaurants gravitate towards the former marshland of the leafy French Concession, Shanghai's most charming neighbourhood. The former stamping ground of crooks, adventurers, writers and gangsters, including the infamous gang boss 'Big Ears' Du Yue-sheng, the French Concession was also the site of Shanghai's first riot in 1874, provoked by a French municipal council decision to plough a road through a Chinese cemetery. Radical opinion flourished on the streets and the **Chinese Communist Party** was conceived here in 1921 (p27).

Cruisin' the tree-lined streets of the French Concession

Wander the French Concession in low gear for its unique flavours by taking the walking tour (p36). Shopping needs are resourcefully met along bustling **Central Huaihai Rd** – usefully punctuated by metro stations – which neatly clips the concession into north and south. Famed for its malls and department stores, Central Huaihai Rd is similarly celebrated for boisterous **Xiangyang Market**, Shanghai's premier outdoor shopping stop. While navigating Central Huaihai Rd, note the Art Deco form of the old **Cathay Theatre** cinema on the corner of South Maoming Rd, and take stock of old apartment blocks such as the **Astrid Apartments** – where well-heeled foreigners lived in the 1920s and 30s.

Almost the exact opposite of kit-built Pudong, the charming enclave of the French Concession guarantees the district the greatest concentration of eateries, bars, nightclubs and sheer style in town. Eat, drink and shop at exclusively smart and elegant **Xintiandi**, peruse the **former homes** of the 'Father of Modern China', **Sun Yatsen** and his wife **Song Qingling**, get lost in a creative maze of galleries and shops at the **Taikang Rd Art Centre** and sleep it all off in one of the many historic hotels.

INFORMATION

Ⓜ South Huangpi Rd; South Shaanxi Rd; Changshu Rd; Hengshan Rd

XINTIANDI 新天地 (3, H2)

By far the city's snappiest zone of restaurants, cafés, bars and small shops, this French Concession complex of restored *shíkùmén* (stone-gate house) households hoists Shanghai into a further dimension of style. Some of Shanghai's best **restaurants** have taken up residence here since Xintiandi's inception in 2001, including T8, Va Bene, Kabb and beyond. Alongside the snappy restaurant scene a gaggle of designer bars serve as useful watering holes, while the huge **UME International Cineplex** takes care of rainy days. The downside is Xintiandi's exclusivity, making a night on its immaculate tiles an expensive proposition for all but the sturdiest of wallets.

The name Xintiandi (literally New Heaven and Earth) is a fanciful invention by developers, a contrivance that, despite its authentic restored *shíkùmén* housing, goes to the heart of this fusion of traditional Shanghai and modern marketing. Xintiandi's particular charms undoubtedly flow from the stone harmonies of its *shíkùmén* architecture, so earmark a visit to the **Shikumen Open House Museum** for a low-down on the local architectural vernacular. You will probably want to slowly saunter through this trendy enclave, but take time to pop your head into the **Site of the 1st National Congress of the Chinese Communist Party**, surreally lodged in one corner of this fashionable enclave. If Mao Zedong had glanced into his crystal ball, he could well have put his money into real estate, or opened a fusion restaurant instead.

INFORMATION

- 🖥 www.xintiandi.com
- ✉ cnr Taicang Rd & Madang Rd
- Ⓜ South Huangpi Rd
- ♿ OK

Representative of Xintiandi's exclusivity, the private club One Xintiandi

HUANGPU RIVER CRUISE 黄浦江游览 (5, J5)

Neatly cleaving Shanghai into two distinct geographical and psychological entities – Puxi and Pudong – the Huangpu River has long been the city's lifeblood. The Huangpu River cruise affords a scenic assessment of Shanghai's two incompatible personas – **the Bund** and **Lujiazui** in Pudong – while ferrying visitors as far as the mouth of the mighty **Yangzi River** (Changjiang), whose waters originate high up on the Qinghai–Tibetan plateau – part of China perhaps, but a world away on any geographic or cultural scale.

The Bund's hallmark sights – the HSBC Building, the Customs House and the Peace Hotel – can all be savoured, before the ferry drifts past Waibaidu (Garden) Bridge, with the brick form of Broadway Mansions just to the west. The eye-catching verticality of Pudong to the east is a glass-and-steel confirmation of Shanghai's vitality. If it gets the go-ahead, the world's largest Ferris wheel (230m high) may be revolving above Hongkou by 2008. Short night cruises are recommended for the neon backdrop of Pudong and the illuminated grandeur of the Bund.

> ### WAIBAIDU BRIDGE 外白渡桥
> Before 1856, the crossing of Suzhou Creek had to be made by ferry as no bridge existed. The first structure to span Suzhou Creek was the wooden Wills Bridge, named after the British engineer who built it. A charge was levied for crossing the bridge, which was later replaced by a pontoon bridge, before the current steel bridge – called Garden Bridge in those days – was erected in 1907.

Shanghai is China's largest port, so the Huangpu River is lined with busy wharves and consequently thick with crafts of every description. The 60km return cruise to **Wusongkou**, the mouth of the Yangzi River, takes 3½ hours and offers a variety of ticket prices and classes (from Y70 to Y120). Briefer trips are also offered for views of the vast **Yangpu** and **Nanpu** bridges (Y45), among the world's longest cable-stayed bridges, if time is tight. Popular 30-minute cruises also depart hourly from the Pearl Dock in Lujiazui. Night boats cruise to Lupu Bridge – the world's longest steel arch bridge – in the south (from Y35; 7.30pm & 9pm).

The river trip is big business. Eleven different companies and 28 boats offer tours along the Huangpu River – including improvised, creaking old ferries – with new vessels constantly coming on stream.

INFORMATION

☎ 6374 4461
✉ 219-239 First East Zhongshan Rd
$ Y25-Y120
Ⓜ Middle Henan Rd

International Convention Centre, Huangpu

QIBAO 七宝 (1, B2)

In Shanghai's Minhang district, well within reach of the centre of town, the ancient canal town of Qibao – 'Seven Treasures' – dates back to the Northern Song dynasty (AD 960–1127). Reaching its apogee during the Ming and Qing dynasties, Qibao is littered with traditional historic architecture, threaded by small busy alleyways and cut by a picturesque canal. A trip to Qibao brings one closer to the real China – with its grittier textures and vestiges of traditional village life, including wooden bucket makers and inquisitive locals. The town has been successfully commercialised for the Chinese market, but considerable ancient architecture and the original layout survives.

The **Qibao Temple** is largely modern, but hunt down the fabulous **Catholic Church**, next to a convent off Qibao Nanjie, south of the canal. The single-spire edifice (☎ 6479 9317; 50 Nanjie; ✝ mass held Sunday 7.30am) dates back to 1867 – pop inside and admire the bright, white-washed interior, confessional, small shuttered windows and attractively painted ceiling. Traversed by arched bridges, the canal bisects Qibao and half-hour **boat rides** (per person Y10; depart 8.30am to 4.30pm) slowly ferry passengers along the picturesque route from **Number One Bridge** to **Dongtangtan** and back.

If souvenir hunting, wander up **Bei Dajie** north of the canal, stuffed with small shops and admire the traditional architecture. Several other sights are scattered through Qibao– including the **Opera House**, the **Cotton Spinning and Weaving Workshop** and the **Qibao Distillery Workshop** – but a slow wander around the alleyways works best. Round off the day with a meal at one of a plethora of **small eateries**, all offering the full gamut of cooking styles from northeast cuisine to Xinjiang and Japanese. A ticket office officially exists at the entrance to Qibao, but is sometimes shut, so just wander in. A taxi from the centre of town will cost around Y55.

THE JEWS OF SHANGHAI

Kaifeng in Henan province is the ancestral home of indigenous Chinese Jews, but Shanghai has China's greatest collection of immigrant Jewish artifacts. Sephardic Jews, who first came to Shanghai in the mid-19th century, included the Sassoons and the Hardoons. Larger influxes arrived in 1906, with Russian Jews escaping persecution, and between 1933 and 1941, when European Jews fled the Nazis. Hitler tried unsuccessfully to extend the holocaust to China with the cooperation of the Japanese, who instead confined Jews to the ghetto area of Hongkou (Map 2, C1), where Jewish monuments survive to this day. The **Tour of Jewish Shanghai** (www.shanghai-jews.com) offers a comprehensive tour.

Sights & Activities

NOTABLE BUILDINGS

Central Shanghai is replete with its distinctive and eye-catching architecture, from the historical villas of the French Concession to the pompous neo-classical façades on the Bund, while not ignoring the impetuous modernity of Pudong.

Customs House
海关 (5, J4)
Constructed in 1927, the imposing Customs House is topped by a clock tower encasing Big Ching, a bell modelled on Big Ben. Wander into the lobby to examine its ceiling mosaics of Chinese junks and maritime vessels. The former customs jetty was located by the Huangpu River on the opposite side of the road.
✉ 13 First East Zhongshan Rd Ⓜ Middle Henan Rd ♿ poor

Dajing Pavilion
大境阁 (5, H6)
Beijing's mighty Ming dynasty city walls were felled in the 1950s, while the fate of Shanghai's smaller 5km-long bastion was sealed soon after the toppling of the Manchu Qing – the architects of this surviving chunk of masonry.
✉ 269 Dajing Rd 💲 Y5 🕐 9am-4pm Ⓜ Middle Henan Rd

Hengshan Moller Villa
衡山马勒别墅 (3, E1)
An ornate and whimsical marvel in the French Concession, the Hengshan Moller Villa dates back to 1936.

ROAD NAMES
In Beijing – and other large cities in China – street signs simply provide the Chinese characters and *pīnyīn*. It may not be English, but *pīnyīn* is readily legible to most Western eyes.

Shanghai has to be different, and enters the fray with a confounding system of English translations to street names, further confused by variant spellings and the absence of an overall standard. It's quite possible to see 淮海中路 transliterated as Huaihai Middle Rd, Central Huaihai Rd, Huaihai Zhonglu or Huai Hai Zhong Lu. To further addle visitors, you may still see old English transliterations (eg Hwashan Rd). In this book, we have listed street names as they appear on street signs.

Designed by wealthy Swede Eric Moller for a daughter who longed for a fairytale castle, the building was requisitioned by Japanese troops in 1941 before later housing a nest of Kuomintang spies. After a long spell serving as the headquarters of the Chinese Communist Youth League, the villa was converted into a hotel and is a fine place to sink an espresso at one of the lawn side Bonomi Café tables, or even book a room.
☎ 6247 8881 💻 www.mollervilla.com ✉ 30 South Shaanxi Rd Ⓜ Shimen No 1 Rd/Jing'an Temple/South Shaanxi Rd

Hong Kong & Shanghai Bank (HSBC) Building
汇丰银行遗址 (5, J4)
One of the Bund's signature sights, the HSBC is the most famous building on the waterfront after the Peace Hotel. At the time of its construction in 1923, it was the world's second largest bank building. Now rented out to the Pudong Development Bank, the bank contains many original features, including fabulous ceiling mosaics. You can also go upstairs to the Bonomi Café.
✉ 12 First East Zhongshan Rd Ⓜ Middle Henan Rd ♿ poor

Dome mosaics of HSBC Building

Jinmao Tower

金茂大厦 (6, 3C)

A glittering section of Art Deco-inspired stainless steel, the Jinmao is China's tallest tower. Approaching the building, spot the 'no climbing' notices at the foot of the 421m-high tower (in case you are tempted). Don't fret, there are other ways up and high-speed elevators can shuttle you to the 88th floor observation deck (Y50) in under a minute. Visitors wishing to dwell longer can check into the Grand Hyatt (p70) on the upper floors.

✉ 88 Century Blvd
💲 Y50 ⏱ 8.30am-10pm
Ⓜ Lujiazui

Jinmao Tower, Pudong

Oriental Pearl TV Tower

东方明珠广播电视塔 (6, 3B)

Without its basement Shanghai Municipal History Museum (p26), this poured-concrete shocker of a tripod tower – with its Byzantine ticket pricing system and artless nod to 1950s sci-fi character, Dan Dare – would signal the triumph of marketing over substance. If stratospheric views over Shanghai tops your list of must-dos then you can patiently queue for the lift to the top spheroid in this love-it-or-hate-it tower – alternatively visit the more spectacular Jinmao Tower down the road.

☎ 5879 1888 ✉ 2 Lujiazui Rd 💲 Y35-150 ⏱ 8.30am-9.30pm Ⓜ Lujiazui
🚌 sightseeing bus No 3 from Shanghai Stadium
♿ OK

Peace Hotel

和平饭店 (5, 3J)

Nowhere suggests Shanghai's Art Deco past more extravagantly than the Peace Hotel. Stooge around the lobby to see who's checking in, take in the ceiling and

Oriental Pearl TV Tower

period features and hunt out the stained glass up the stairs at the back. Or stay in one of the rooms (p72).

☎ 6321 6888 ✉ 20 East Nanjing Rd 🖥 www.shanghaipeacehotel.com Ⓜ Middle Henan Rd ♿ OK

Shanghai Exhibition Centre

上海展览中心 (5, B6)

While doing West Nanjing Rd, put aside some time to weigh up the ponderous exterior of this overblown Soviet edifice opposite the Shanghai Centre. A frequent venue for large-scale exhibitions, the building serves as a monument to socialist aesthetics: there was a time when Pudong was set to look like this.

✉ 1000 Central Yan'an Rd
Ⓜ Jing'an Temple

Shanghai Exhibition Centre

THAT SINKING FEELING

The Shanghai skyline may be rising faster than any other, but even way back in the 1920s local geologists noted that Shanghai was slowly sinking into its spongy foundations. A combination of excessive water extraction and feverish high-rise construction now has Shanghai sinking at an annual rate of 1.5cm. With thousands of towering buildings in the crowded pipeline, experts warn of further land subsidence and cave-ins. As skyscraper construction is a patchy business, areas are not sinking at uniform rates, although this could be inconsequential, as sea levels rise. Shanghai – Paris of the Orient or Venice of the East?

FORMER RESIDENCES

Former Residence of Lu Xun
鲁迅故居 (2, C1)
Lu Xun buffs will adore ferreting around this simple three-floor domicile on lovely Shanyin Rd, where an English-speaking guide can fill you in on the bits and bobs, including a clock displaying the time of Lu Xun's death and a painting of the writer's baby son Zhou Haiying on the wall.
✉ 9, Lane 132, Shanyin Rd ⑤ Y8 ⏱ 9am-4pm Ⓜ Hongkou Stadium light rail

Song Qingling's Former Residence
宋庆龄故居 (3, B5)
Awful pebbledash exterior aside, the period furnishings at this former home of the wife of Dr Sun Yatsen are worth a peek, but it's the English-style garden at the rear, with its lawn, *Magnolia grandiflora* and towering camphor trees, that steals the show. Has English captions.
☎ 6474 7183 ✉ 1843 Huaihai Middle Rd ⑤ adult/student Y8/4 ⏱ 9am-4.30pm Ⓜ Hengshan Rd

Stony faced, Song Qinglong at her former residence

The 'Father of Modern China', Sun Yatsen's former residence

Sun Yatsen's Former Residence
孙中山故居 (3, G3)
Erstwhile Shanghai home of the father of modern China *(guófù)*, this two-storey dwelling is a simple and retiring slice of Sun Yatsen (aka Sun Zhongshan; 1866–1925) nostalgia and memorabilia.
☎ 6437 2954 ✉ 7 Xiangshan Rd ⑤ Y8 ⏱ 9am-4.30pm Ⓜ South Shaanxi Rd

Zhou Enlai's Former Residence
周恩来故居 (3, G3)
The Shanghai home to ex-Premier Zhou Enlai, whose death in 1976 sparked anti–Gang of Four riots in Beijing known as the Tiananmen Incident, this three-storey villa is typically Spartan in appearance, but is located in a charming area.
☎ 6473 0420 ✉ 73 Sinan Rd ⑤ Y2 ⏱ 9am-4pm Ⓜ South Shaanxi Rd

TEMPLES AND PLACES OF WORSHIP

Shanghai's temples and shrines open a window onto the city's spiritual realm, where age old Chinese traditions survive amid the city's immigrant faiths that have erected mosques, churches and synagogues as places of contemplation and worship.

Baiyun Temple
白云观 (4, A1)
Neither as large nor as magnificent as its counterpart in Beijing, the centrepiece of this recently relocated, modern port-red temple is the main hall with its vast seated effigy of the Jade Emperor (Yuhuang Dadi). The drum and bell can be found upstairs, along with the Hall to the God of Wealth and other shrines to lesser deities.
✉ 239 Dajing Rd ⑤ Y2 ⏱ 9am-5pm Ⓜ South Huangpi Rd

Chenxiangge Nunnery
沉香阁 (4, B1)
This quaint Old Town nunnery has some fascinating touches, such as the androgynous statue of the Maitreya Buddha as you enter (in place of the usual, chubby Milefo), enchanting yellow walls, its mantra-murmuring contingent of brown-robed nuns and a fabulous effigy of Guanyin upstairs in the building at the rear.
☎ 6328 7884 ✉ 29 Chenxiangge Rd ⑤ Y5 ⏱ 7am-4pm Ⓜ Middle Henan Rd

BELLYFUL OF LAUGHS

Facing south and greeting worshippers in the first hall of Chinese Buddhist temples is the rotund and golden form of Milefo, the Laughing Buddha. The big-bellied character – also called the monk with the cloth bag *(bùdài héshang)* – is actually a popular representation of the bodhisattva (a Buddha-to-be) Maitreya, the Future Buddha. His fat form commemorates an actual monk and native of Zhejiang province from the 10th century, believed to be the embodiment of Maitreya Buddha.

Confucian Temple
文庙 (4, A2)

This excellent shrine originally dates from 1294, but was moved to this site in 1855. A delightful and well-cultivated temple, this sanctuary of Confucian ideals is much better tended than many of China's other temples to Kongzi. Bibliophiles can leaf through the second-hand book market here on Sundays.
✉ 215 Wenmiao Rd
$ Y10 🕐 9am-5pm (last tickets 4.30pm) Ⓜ South Huangpi Rd

Dongjiadu Catholic Church
董家渡天主堂 (2, C2)

Dating back to 1853, when the Taiping Rebellion was in full swing, the Spanish-styled Jesuit-built basilica was once named after St Francis Xavier.
✉ 185 Dongjiadu Rd
🕐 services 7am Mon-Sat, 6am Sun

Fazangjiang Temple
法藏讲寺 (4, A2)

Unlike most Chinese temples, which you enter through the southern gate, the main door to this temple is curiously

located on the west – clearly a later addition or a temporary measure. At the time of writing, the Great Treasure Hall was being repaired, with a large statue of Sakyamuni seated lily-top and the Hall of Heavenly Kings, in the south, restored but awaiting its statues.
✉ 271 Ji'an Rd 🕐 7.30am-4pm $ Y2 Ⓜ South Huangpi Rd

Hengshan Community Church
国际礼拜堂 (3, D5)

Bustling on Sunday afternoons with expats, this non-denominational church is an excellent place for both visitors and worshippers. With a lovely front garden lawn and a warm sense of welcome, this is one of Shanghai's most pleasant churches.
☎ 6437 6576 ✉ 53 Hengshan Rd 🕐 services held at 7.30am, 10am & 7pm Sun, with English services at 4pm Ⓜ Hengshan Rd

Confucius says pigeon droppings are not appreciated, Confucian Temple

FIGHTING FIT

If you want to brush up on your *white crane shows the way, monkey offers peach* and other electrifying *gōngfu* (kung fu) moves, the **Longwu International Kungfu Centre** (3, F3; ☎ 5465 0042; www.longwukungfu.com; 215 South Shaanxi Rd) has a wide range of martial arts and health systems (*tàijíquán, wing chun, aikido,* yoga and more) that can be studied once off (Y100 per lesson) or in blocks. The smaller **Wuyi Chinese Kungfu Centre** (3, G4; ☎ 1370 168 5893; wuyi_kungfu_centre@yahoo .com; studio 311, Building 3, Lane 201, Taikang Rd) in the Taikang Lu Art Centre has classes in *tàijíquán* and Chinese *wǔshù.*

Bruce Lee wannabes should head to the Longwu International Kungfu Centre

Jing'an Temple
静安寺 (5, A6)
Above the Jing'an Temple metro on West Nanjing Rd, the Jing'an (Tranquil) Temple is a queer fish. Originally dating to AD 247, the temple has been opulently rebuilt in parts – including the impressive front wall – but in place of a main hall you get a flight of concrete steps and a block resembling a nuclear bunker.
☎ 6256 6366 ⊠ 1686 West Nanjing Rd $ Y5
🕑 7.30am-5pm Ⓜ Jing'an Temple

Moore Memorial Church
沐恩堂 (5, F4)
This active red-brick church east of Renmin Square and next to the Yangtze Hotel is a simple and unaffected former Methodist church.
☎ 6322 5069 ⊠ 316 Central Xizang Rd 🕑 6am-7pm Sun Ⓜ Renmin Square

Ohel Moishe Synagogue
摩西会堂 (6, C1)
Built by the Ashkenazi Jewish community in 1927, this defunct synagogue in the former Jewish ghetto has a small museum collection of old photographs. Visits to the synagogue are a feature of the '**Tour of Jewish Shanghai**' (☎ 6278 0225; www.shanghai-jews.com).
☎ 6541 6312 ⊠ 62 Changyang Rd $ Y50
🕑 9am-4.30pm Mon-Fri
🚌 Nos 37, 935 from the Bund

Ohel Rachel Synagogue
犹太教堂 (5, B5)
Facing Jerusalem and built in 1920 by Jacom Sassoon, the ivy-cloaked Ohel Rachel ('House of Rachel') synagogue now houses the very secular Shanghai Education Commission. When it was built, it served as a focal point for the Sephardic Jews of Shanghai but is now rarely used for worship. The temple's time-worn exterior can be admired from the outside, but access is generally not permitted.
⊠ 500 North Shaanxi Rd Ⓜ Shimen No 1 Rd

Sheshan Cathedral
佘山大教堂 (1, B2)
The matriarch of all of Shanghai's churches, this

cruciform Catholic cathedral dominates the scenic area of Sheshan, 30km southwest of Shanghai. A Jesuit accomplishment, the original Holy Mother Cathedral was built here in 1866 and replaced with the current hill-top Basilica of Notre Dame, completed in 1935. A walk up to the church from the south gate takes you past several shrines, or you can take the cable car.
☎ 5765 1521 ✉ Sheshan, Songjiang County 🚌 No 1M from Shanghai Stadium Sightseeing Bus Station (8, B4) 🕐 8am-4pm

Temple of the Town Gods

城隍庙 (4, B1)
A smoky portal to the Taoist metaphysical realm flanked by the frenetic Yuyuan Bazaar, this shrine lapsed into a predictable decline during the dark ages of the Cultural Revolution, but swarms today with worshippers and visitors.
✉ Yuyuan Bazaar $ Y5 🕐 8.30am-4pm M Middle Henan Rd

Xiaotaoyuan Mosque

小桃园清真寺 (4, B2)
Shanghai's largest place of worship for local Muslims, the Xiaotaoyuan ('Little Peach Garden') Mosque consists of a large prayer hall hung with fans (no entry permitted to non-Muslims), and dates from 1930. An ancient and timeworn stele can be found embedded in a wall and the date 1343 above the entrance refers to calculations on the Muslim calendar.
✉ 52 Xiao Taoyuan St

MUSEUMS

With a target of 150 museums by the year 2010, museum space is expanding in Shanghai. All museums have (often quite expensive) entrance fees, but English captions are often either inadequate or absent. At the time of writing a Museum of Modern Art was due to open in Renmin Park in late 2005; the fabulous collection of Chinese artifacts in the Shanghai Museum (p9) is reviewed in the Highlights chapter.

Bund Museum

外滩博物馆 (5, J4)
More notable as a quirky architectural conclusion to the southern foot of the Bund, this small museum – housed in the Meteorological Signal Tower – only aspires to a smattering of old photographs.
☎ 6321 6542 ✉ First East Zhongshan Rd 🕐 9am-6pm $ free M Middle Henan Rd

Duolun Road Cultural Street

多伦文化名人街 (2, C1)
A charming stretch of *shíkùmén* buildings and former habitat of the Shanghai literati, the tourist sights of dolled up and cobbled Duolun Rd include the Shanghai Duolun Museum of Modern Art (p30), the Old Film Café (p58), the Reading Room Café, the Former Residence of Lu Xun (p22) and a gaggle of curio and specialist shops.
M East Baoxing Rd light rail 🚌 No 21 from Suzhou Creek ♿ OK

Lujiazui Development Showroom

陆家嘴开发陈列室 (6, C3)
Don't let the small scattering of drab exhibits and before-and-after photos of modern Lujiazui dissuade you from popping in to eye up the architecture of this traditional Chinese residence dating from 1917, in the shadow of the looming Jinmao Tower.
☎ 5887 9964 ✉ 15 East Lujiazui Rd $ Y5 M Lujiazui

A FACE IN THE CROWD

Han Chinese *(hànzú)* substantially outnumber everyone else in Shanghai, giving the city a largely racially homogenous countenance. Leaving debate of Han Chinese ethnicity aside, the city has long attracted immigrants and settlers from home and abroad. According to official figures, over 50,000 members of minority groups live in Shanghai, including the Muslim Hui and northeastern Manchu, and smaller numbers of Uighurs, Va, Lahu, Jing and other minorities. Commonly employed in menial jobs, the Subei hail from northern Jiangsu and although strictly Han, they are considered a minority group by locals. An astonishing 300,000 Taiwanese live here and even expat numbers run to around 100,000.

Lu Xun Memorial Hall

鲁迅纪念馆 (2, C1)

This excellent museum charts the life and creative output of Lu Xun – China's most celebrated modernist writer – by way of photographs, first editions, waxworks and the author's personal effects. Detailed English captions throughout.

✉ Lu Xun Park, 2288 North Sichuan Rd 🕑 9am-5pm 💲 adult/student Y8/4 Ⓜ Hongkou Stadium light rail

Museum of Folk Art

民间收藏品陈列馆 (2, C2)

A mildly interesting collection of folk art creations, housed in a traditional guildhall. ☎ 6313 5582 ✉ 1551 First South Zhongshan Rd 🕑 9am-4pm 💲 Y4

Museum of Public Security

上海公安博物馆 (2, B2)

The long arm of the Shanghai law is exposed at this French Concession museum, with exhibits featuring a cache of weapons including Sun Yatsen's pistol, machine guns and other firearms. ☎ 6472 0256 ✉ 518 South Ruijin Rd 💲 Y8 🕑 9am-4.30pm Mon-Sat

Shanghai Arts & Crafts Museum

上海工艺美术博物馆 (3, E4)

Set within a gorgeous 1905 villa, this absorbing museum colourfully introduces visitors to traditional Chinese arts such as paper-cutting, embroidery and lantern making. ☎ 6437 3454 ✉ 79 Fenyang Rd 💲 Y8 🕑 9am-5pm Ⓜ Changshu Rd

Shanghai Municipal History Museum

上海城市历史发展陈列馆 (6, B3)

The city's most fascinating collection after the Shanghai Museum, set aside at least a few hours for the excellent

---

OFF THE RAILS

If you need to reach Pudong international airport chop-chop, Shanghai's futuristic Maglev train comes with a top warp speed of 430km/h. In place of conventional wheels, the carriages are suspended above the tracks by a magnetic field. LED meters notch up the rapidly escalating velocity, although the train starts to decelerate around five minutes into the eight-minute journey, in preparation for arrival. Despite a slight wobble, it's a smooth ride, but the track is slowly sinking into marshy Pudong and travellers laden with heavy luggage will curse the long trudge from the Maglev terminus to the metro station at Longyang Rd.

Standing up to the men at Shanghai Municipal History Museum

exhibits here. To get the city's past in perspective, head upstairs for a cobbled walk along Shanghai's old streetscapes and hunt down one of a pair of bronze lions that used to sit outside the HSBC Building on the Bund. The elaborate replica of the Dangui Teahouse is typical of the extraordinary level of detail while the lifelike waxworks come from the hands of skilled artisans. There are English captions throughout (rendering the Y30 audio tour unnecessary).

☎ 5879 8888/3003 ✉ Basement, Oriental Pearl TV Tower, 2 Lujiazui Rd $ Y35 ⏰ 9am-9pm Ⓜ Lujiazui

Shanghai Music Conservatory Oriental Musical Instrument Museum

上海音乐学院东方乐器博物馆 (3, E3)

This excellent museum affords a rare glimpse at China's panoply of musical instruments, including folk and ethnic minority instruments. ☎ 6431 2157 ✉ 20 Fenyang Rd $ Y10 ⏰ 9-11am & 1.30-5pm Ⓜ Changshu Rd

Shanghai Natural History Museum

上海自然博物馆 (5, H5)

Located in the former Cotton Exchange Building, this gloomy building's draw cards are its original architectural features, its horned fossilised bulk of a *Tsintaosaurus* and the ground floor Ming dynasty mummies excavated from Dapu Qiao and Xietu Rd. ✉ 260 East Yan'an Rd $ Y5 ⏰ 9am-4.50pm Tue-Sun Ⓜ Middle Henan Rd

Shanghai Urban Planning Exhibition Hall

上海城市规划展示馆 (5, F5)

Glance into the crystal ball to discern the shape of future Shanghai at this Renmin Square exhibition hall, laid out over five floors. The 3rd-floor model of the city come 2020 is a twinkling, Utopian high-rise vision (impressions of the city after a Chinese invasion of Taiwan, which has threatened retaliatory missile strikes on Shanghai, not represented).

☎ 6318 4477/6372 2077 ✉ 10 Renmin Ave $ Y25 ⏰ 9am-4pm Ⓜ Renmin Square

Shanghai Urban Planning Exhibition Hall

Shikumen Open House Museum

屋里厢石库门民居陈列室 (3, H2)

This worthwhile museum explores the history of this traditional architectural style that characterises much of Xintiandi.

☎ 3307 0337 ✉ 25, Lane 181, North Block, Xintiandi, Taicang Rd $ Y20/10 ⏰ 10am-10pm Ⓜ South Huangpi Rd

Site of the 1st National Congress of the CCP

中共一大会址纪念馆 (3, H2)

Immersed in communist nostalgia, this hallowed site hosted the founding of the Chinese Communist Party (CCP) on 23 July 1921. Caught in a peculiar time warp at the very nub of CCP self-glorification while serving as a Xintiandi cornerstone, the museum's chest-thumping should flag it as a mere curiosity, but its historical significance is undeniable.

☎ 5383 2171 ✉ 76-78 Xingye Rd, Xintiandi $ Y3 ⏰ 9am-4pm Ⓜ South Huangpi Rd

DISCOUNT TICKETS

A combined ticket costing Y60 (valid for one day only) exists for sights in Renmin Square, including admission to the Shanghai Museum, the Shanghai Art Museum and either the Shanghai Grand Theatre or the Shanghai Urban Planning Exhibition Hall. Alternatively, a combined Shanghai Art Museum and Shanghai Urban Planning Exhibition Hall ticket costs Y45. Several sights in Pudong are also combined on one ticket; eg the Oriental Pearl TV Tower and the Bund Sightseeing Tunnel (Y78) or the Bund Sightseeing Tunnel and the Shanghai Science and Technology Museum (Y90).

SHANGHAI FOR CHILDREN

The Chinese love children dearly and pay them attention verging on adulation, so be prepared for your adorable moppets to be coddled at every turn by wide-eyed *āyí* (aunties) and *shūshu* (uncles). Shanghai is well-equipped if you have little ones in tow and you can find all the parenting paraphernalia you may need. Baby-changing rooms are rare, and very cheap restaurants won't have child seats. An excellent day trip for families is Shanghai Zoo (p12). Your kids may see the Bund and the Shanghai Museum as the *ne plus ultra* of boredom, so steer them in the following direction.

Changfeng Ocean World

长风海底世界 (2, A2)
Adults may find this subterranean aquarium dank, dark, dingy and dear, but the little people will adore the clown fish, shark tunnel and (tacky) sea lion/white whale shows. Attention parents with strollers – the lift bypassing the slog down the stairs *may* or *may not* work.
⊠ Gate No 4, Changfeng Park, 451 Daduhe Rd
🕑 Y110/80

Deep Sea World

深海珍奇展 (6, A3)
This rather cheap-looking aquarium is not worth it as a stand-alone, but kids may get a kick from the Bund Sightseeing Tunnel (p32) which comes on a combined ticket with this aquarium. The cowfish – with horn-like protrusions – are unusual, while the clownfish go down well with Pixar fans.
⊠ Bund Sightseeing Tunnel (Pudong end) $ Y30
🕑 8am-10.30pm Mon-Thu, 8am-10pm Fri-Sun
Ⓜ Lujiazui/Middle Henan Rd

Dino Beach 热带风暴

Pack the water wings, swimming trunks and waterproof sun-cream for fun family frolicking at this water park.
☎ 6478 3333 ⊠ 78 Xinzhen Rd $ Mon-Fri Y120, Sat & Sun Y150
🕑 9am-9pm Jun-Sep (later mid-July to mid-Aug)
🚌 shuttle bus from Shanghai Stadium

Hengshan Community Church

国际礼拜堂 (3, D5)
This gorgeous church (p23) has a variety of Sunday school classes for children of various ages and a tots nursery downstairs on Sundays.
☎ 6437 6576 ⊠ 53 Hengshan Rd 🕑 services held in English 4pm Sun
Ⓜ Hengshan Rd

Pottery Workshop Shanghai

上海乐天陶社 (3, G4)
A cornerstone of the Taikang Rd Art Centre, the upstairs-workshop stages creative pottery classes for both adults and kids, with instruction from qualified potters. The children's class (English and Chinese) is on Saturdays from 10am to 11am.
☎ 6445 0902 🖳 www .ceramics.com.hk ⊠ 2nd fl, 220 Taikang Rd 🕑 10am-6pm Ⓜ South Shaanxi Rd

Why play the real thing, when you can play virtual soccer at Science & Technology Museum

Shanghai Aquarium

上海海洋水族馆 (6, B2)
Ideal for infant marine biologists, this Pudong aquarium near the Oriental Pearl TV Tower is Shanghai's best and brings you and your little ones face to face with a galaxy of brightly coloured sea creatures. The 155m-long glass tunnel is the draw card sight, eliciting gasps and finger-pointing. Fish feedings are a further crowd puller.
☎ 5877 9988 🖳 www .aquarium.sh.cn ✉ 158 North Yincheng Rd 💲 adult/ senior/child Y110/65/70 🕑 9am-9pm 🚇 Lujiazui

Shanghai Natural Wild Insect Kingdom

上海大自然野生昆虫馆 (6, A3)
Your little ones can give creepy crawlies the once over at this Sino-Singaporean bug zoo, a stick insect's throw from the Oriental Pearl TV Tower. Some of the exhibits are hands-on, although your cherubs may want to pass on the hairy, outsize arachnid handlings.
☎ 5840 6950 ✉ 1 Fenghe Rd 💲 Y35/20 🕑 9am-5pm 🚇 Lujiazui

Shanghai Science and Technology Museum

上海科技馆
One of Shanghai's top family diversions, this interactive science museum is intelligently divided into thematic sections, guiding your little boffins on a tour of earth's geology, the natural world, the realm of physics and all the thrills of IMAX 3D movies. Weekend visits can be crowded.
☎ 6862 2000 🖳 www .sstm.org.cn/howyi ✉ 2000

A ROAD BY ANY OTHER NAME

The street names of central Shanghai are largely named – as in other Chinese cities – after the cities and provinces of China. Below are some of Shanghai's former street names:

• Huaihai Rd	Ave Joffre
• Xinhua Rd	Amherst Rd
• West Nanjing Rd	Bubbling Well Rd
• Xiangshan Rd	Rue Moliere
• Jinling Rd	Ave Foch
• Jiangsu Rd	Edinburgh Rd
• Jinshan Rd	Astor Rd
• Tongren Rd	Hardoon Rd
• East Yan'an Rd	Edward VII Avenue
• Fenyang Rd	Rue Pichon
• Gaolan Rd	Rue Corneille
• Panyu Rd	Columbia Rd
• Guangdong Rd	Canton Rd

Century Blvd 💲 adult/child under 1.2m/over 1.2 m Y60/20/40 🕑 9am-5.30pm (last tickets sold at 3.30pm) Tue-Sun 🚇 Shanghai Science and Technology Museum

Shanghai Wild Animal Park

上海野生动物园 (1, C2)
Out in the sticks, this park is home to a diverse menagerie of feral beasts from white rhinoceros (the second largest species of land mammal), to south China tigers, Manchurian tigers, giraffes, kangaroos, lions, bears, elephants and more. Visitors are driven through the grounds in vehicles, so there's no need to pack the tranquiliser darts (although a handler was mauled to death several years back after leaving his vehicle).
☎ 5803 6000 (phone for opening times) ✉ Sanzhao, Nanhui District 💲 adult/child

---

(under 1.2m) Y80/40 🚌 Shanghai sightseeing bus line No 2 from Shanghai Stadium

Tom's World 汤姆熊 (5, G4)

If your kids are protesting at your shopping exploits, bring them here to this buzzing, clicking and bleeping basement amusement arcade on East Nanjing Rd. Tickets you win on games are redeemable for prizes at the desk.
✉ 673 East Nanjing Rd 🕑 10am-11pm 🚇 Renmin Park/Middle Henan Rd

Zhongshan Park

中山公园 (2, A2)
Within this park is Fundazzle, an excellent adventure playground, where tiny tots can take to bouncing castles, slides and mazes.
✉ 780 Changning Rd 💲 Y2; Fundazzle Y25 🕑 6am-6pm 🚇 Zhongshan Park ♿ OK

ART GALLERIES

In certain neighbourhoods, art galleries are as common as *xiǎomàibù* (family stores) as entrepreneurs try to cash in on the burgeoning taste for paintings. The market is flooded with garish, chocolate-box style landscapes, but more experimental art work can be found at the following galleries.

Art Scene China
艺术景画廊 (3, C4)
Ensconced in a 1930s villa, this charming gallery showcases contemporary works by the 25 artists it promotes, and operates a helpful website.
☎ 6437 0631 🖳 www .artscenechina.com ✉ No 8, Lane 37, West Fuxing Rd ⏲ 10.30am-7.30pm Ⓜ Changshu Rd

Deke Erh Centre
尔冬强艺术中心 (3, G4)
Photographer and acting curator for the city of Shanghai, Deke Erh's gallery is a component of the Taikang Rd Art Centre.
☎ 6415 0675 🖳 www .han-yuan.com ✉ Lane 210, 2 Taikang Rd

50 Moganshan Rd
莫干山路50号 (5, B2)
West over Suzhou Creek from the Shanghai Train Station is this excellent warren of art galleries, cafés, shops and design studios, with views over vessels chugging along the river. Aim to spend half a day here, perusing some invigorating art work at ShanghART, the New Red Door Gallery, Eastlink Gallery and other top galleries, sip a coffee at Bandu Cabin (p57) and load up with stylised furniture at Art Deco.
✉ 50 Moganshan Rd ⏲ 10.30am-6pm Ⓜ Shanghai Train Station

Shanghai Duolun Museum of Modern Art
多伦现代美术馆 (2, C1)
With artists in residence and an electrifying focus on contemporary art, this excellent museum brings cutting edge art and a graeat range of art books to Duolun Rd Cultural Street (p25).
☎ 6587 6902 🖳 www .duolunart.com ✉ 27 Duolon Rd 💲 Y10 ⏲ 9am-5pm Ⓜ East Baoxing Rd light rail ♿ OK

Room with a View
顶层画廊 (5, G4)
Doubling as an arty bar, this gallery showcases contemporary art, photography and film screenings.
☎ 6352 0256 🖳 www .topart.cn ✉ 12th fl, 479 East Nanjing Rd ⏲ 3.30-10pm Ⓜ Middle Henan Rd

ShanghART
香格纳画廊 (5, B2)
A major component of 50 Moganshan Rd (left), this gallery has two huge warehouse spaces showcasing exciting local talent. Click on the useful website for full details and a calendar of upcoming exhibitions.
☎ 6359 3923 ✉ building 16 & 18, 50 Moganshan Rd 🖳 www.shanghartgallery .com ⏲ 10am-7pm Ⓜ Shanghai Train Station ♿ poor

Shanghai Art Museum

Shanghai Art Museum
上海美术馆 (5, E5)
A lovely, spacious museum with superb exhibition halls – especially the ground floor hall – the building itself is as worth exploring as the well-illuminated art work. A major drawback of this art museum is the sporadic English captions, defying the legions of Western visitors that traipse through.
☎ 6327 2829 ✉ 325 West Nanjing Rd ⏲ 9am-5pm (last entry 4pm) 💲 Y20 Ⓜ Renmin Park ♿ good

Shanghai Gallery of Art
外滩三号沪申画廊 (5, J4)
In keeping with its companion sophisticates at this exclusive Bund address, the spacious Shanghai Gallery of Art regularly stages fresh exhibitions in a challenging array of creative media, from experimental music to sculpture and contemporary art.
☎ 6323 4549 🖳 www .threeonthebund.com ✉ 3rd fl, Three on the Bund, 3 First East Zhongshan Rd ⏲ 11am-11pm Tue-Sun Ⓜ Middle Henan Rd ♿ OK

PARKS & GARDENS

The urban side of Shanghai can be relentless, but parks – often with historical associations and popular with Chinese practising *tàijíquán* (supreme ultimate boxing) or *qìgōng* (breathing exercises) – are strategically located around town.

Fuxing Park
复兴公园 (3, G3)
A pleasant and leafy French Concession enclave, Fuxing Park is laid out with a diverse jumble of trees, anachronistic, stony-faced statues of Karl Marx and Friedrich Engels, slow-motion *tàijíquán* practitioners and a small children's playground.
✉ 2 Gaolan Rd $ Y2 ☻ 6am-6pm M South Huangpi Rd ♿ OK ♨

Gongqing Forest Park
共青森林公园
Shanghai's parks may be largely synthetic spaces with little grass, but this magnificent expanse on the western shore of the Huangpu River is a tranquil slice of countryside in the heart of town. On top of river views, the huge array of facilities includes a football pitch, fishing, boating, horse riding, a roller coaster and an adventure playground. A guesthouse is at hand for overnighters (Y400).
☎ 6532 8194 🖳 www.gqsl.com $ Y12 ☻ 6am-5pm M Jiangwenzhen light rail station 🚍 tour bus No 8 from Shanghai Stadium (stopping at the Bund and Renmin Square) ♿ OK ♨

Jing'an Park
静安公园 (3, D2)
Across the way from the Jing'an Temple, this pleasant park provides a green and welcome detour off the main Nanjing Rd drag. Early birds can limber up in slow motion with fellow *tàijíquán* and *qìgōng* practitioners.
✉ 189 Huashan Rd M Jing'an Temple ♿ OK

Lu Xun Park
鲁迅公园 (2, C1)
Named after China's foremost 20th-century writer, this huge park is gorgeous in spring and summer, when huge lilies rise from the waters and the trees are in blossom. Lu Xun is buried here and is further commemorated by the Lu Xun Memorial Hall (p26) within the park.
☎ 6306 1181 ✉ 146 East Jiangwan Rd $ Y2 ☻ 9am-5pm M Hongkou Stadium light rail ♿ OK

Renmin Park
人民公园 (5, F5)
Back in the good old bad old days, this park was the site of the racecourse. Today it lies perched at the north end of Renmin Square, its signature clock tower (now the Shanghai Art Museum) overshadowed by the futuristic form of Tomorrow Square.
✉ 231 West Nanjing Rd $ Y2 ☻ 6am-6pm M Renmin Park/Renmin Square ♿ OK

Riverside Promenade
滨江大道 (6, A3)
Hands down the best stroll in Pudong, an amble along the 2.5km-long promenade on the eastern bank of the Huangpu River is punctuated with cafés and accompanied by choice views to the grey edifices on the Bund.
✉ Lujiazui Rd ☻ 6.30am-11pm M Lujiazui ♿ OK

Shanghai Botanic Gardens
上海植物园 (2, B3)
These gardens, 2km southwest of the Longhua Temple, are a refreshing escape from Shanghai's synthetic cityscape. There's an adventure playground, dodgem cars, bike hire and a bouncing castle for the kids. Alternatively, jump on an electronic buggy for a tour.
☎ 6451 3369 ✉ 997 Longwu Rd $ Y15; through ticket Y40 ☻ 6am-6pm ♿ OK ♨

Century Park
世纪公园
It's synthetic and contrived, but this vast park at the conclusion of Century Blvd adds a welcome splash of green to the cold glass, steel and tile textures of Pudong and kids can run riot (with both bike hire and boat hire for playful bobbing about on the lake).
✉ 1001 Jinxiu Rd $ Y10 ☻ 7am-6pm M Century Park ♿ OK

Lotus pond, Lu Xun Park

QUIRKY SHANGHAI

Propaganda Poster Art Centre

宣传画艺术中心 (3, B3)
Propaganda buffs and art historians will go dewy-eyed and weak-kneed perusing this collection of original works from the golden age of Communist mind-control (some are for sale). Ask to be steered to the 'big character posters' (*dàzìbào*), a rare survivor and worth a bob or two. Is located in the basement of Building M around the rear.
☎ 6211 1845 ✉ Room B-OC, 868 Huashan Rd (the guards should show you the way) $ Y20 ⏲ 10am-3pm Ⓜ Changshu Rd

Bund Sightseeing Tunnel

外滩观光隧道 (5, J3)
Cheap props, budget light effects, tacky ghosts, cringe-

Plenty of collectibles at the Propaganda Poster Art Centre

worthy voice-overs — Shanghai's gaudiest attraction, a stupefying 647m-long voyage of flashing lights under the Huangpu River — is so awful it has to be seen. A Y55 ticket includes entry to the excellent China Sex Culture Museum, Deep Sea World and Sound Fantastic World.
✉ The Bund/Lujiazui Rd ⏲ 8am-10.30pm Mon-Thu, 8am-10pm Fri-Sun $ Y30, return Y50
Ⓜ Middle Henan Rd/Lujiazui

China Sex Culture Museum

中华性文化和性健康教育展 (6, A3)
This fascinating foray into Chinese sexuality and erotica has some riveting pieces: hunt down the knife used for castrating eunuchs (punishment for adulterous women), the donkey saddle with the wooden penis, early Chinese books on sex education and the special coins once used as *quid pro quo* in China's brothels of yore.
✉ Bund Sightseeing Tunnel (Lujiazui end) $ Y20 ⏲ 8am-10.30pm Mon-Thu, 8am-10pm Fri-Sun Ⓜ Middle Henan Rd/Lujiazui

THE SHANGHAI DIALECT

Spoken by 13 million people, the Shanghainese dialect belongs to the Wu dialect, named after the kingdom of Wu in present day Jiangsu province. Generally classified as a dialect of Chinese, Shanghainese is considered a separate language by some linguists. To both Mandarin and Cantonese speakers, Shanghainese sounds odd, perhaps because it is a more archaic branch of Chinese. Furthermore, the tonal system of Shanghaihua differs considerably from Mandarin and Cantonese, displaying closer affinities to African tonal languages. A marked Japanese sound to the Shanghai dialect can also be heard. Due to the increasing prevalence of Mandarin and the absence of a standard form of Shanghaihua, the dialect is constantly changing and differs greatly from how it was spoken a few generations ago. If you want to listen to examples of Shanghainese, click on mwc.zanhe.com.

Defiant Nanjing Rd sculpture

Trips & Tours

WALKING TOURS
The Bund 外滩

Choose a weekday – ideally morning – for this walk, when crowds are less fierce. From the **Russian Consulate** (**1**), with its red tiles and patina-green turret flying the Russian flag, wander across the road to the historic **Pujiang Hotel** (**2**; p74), whose guests have included the likes of Albert Einstein (Room 304) and Charlie Chaplin (Room 404). Cross the road to the Orwellian **Broadway Mansions** (**3**) before traversing the steel **Waibaidu Bridge** (**4**; p18) over Suzhou Creek. On the south side of the bridge, turn right under the flyover to the former **British Consulate** (**5**) peaking through the foliage at No 33 First East Zhongshan Rd. At No 29 is the former Banque de L'Indo-China, while south of the Chinese-roofed **Bank of China building** (**6**) rises the patina pyramid of the iconic **Peace Hotel** (**7**; p21), which is worth investigation for its Art Deco stained glass and lobby features. Inspect the lobby mosaics of the distinctive clock-towered

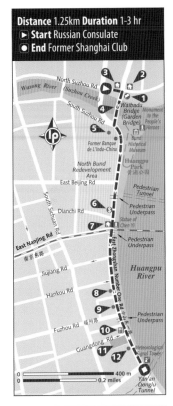

Distance 1.25km **Duration** 1-3 hr
▶ **Start** Russian Consulate
● **End** Former Shanghai Club

Old world interior of Peace Hotel, the Bund

ROAD RUNNER

Shanghai's roads are a clear and present danger. If crossing the road, utilise your peripheral vision at all times and prepare to sprint. The green man doesn't mean it is safe to cross, with cars having right of way in all situations. Vehicles drive along dark streets at dusk with their lights off (occasionally devoid of number plates), honking and sauntering through red lights. Don't expect to find sanctuary on the pavement, where motorbikes, scooters and bicycles plough past pedestrians. China leads the world in road deaths (600 daily, according to World Health Organisation figures), despite having relatively few cars.

Shanghai Customs House (**8**; p20) at No 13, alongside the landmark **Hong Kong and Shanghai Bank Corporation (HSBC) Building** (**9**) at No 12, crowned by its large dome and dating from 1923. Pop inside and crane your neck to survey the fabulous mosaics or sip a coffee at the 2nd-floor Bonomi Café (p52). The terrace of **M on the Bund** (**10**; p49) offers tantalising views and fine food, while further south at No 3 is **Three on the Bund** (**11**), formerly the Union Insurance Company Building, a swish assortment of celebrated restaurants and luxury shops. The former site of the exclusive **Shanghai Club** (**12**) is at No 2, where the club's patrons came to prop up the 33m-long bar, the world's longest in its day. Walk back north along the Bund promenade for long views over to Pudong.

Revolutionary relief at Bund Customs House

Old Town 南市老城

Begin by exploring the **Fuyou Antiques Market** (**1**; p41) and Central Fang-bang Rd before traversing Old Jiaochang Rd and turning left into the **Yuyuan Bazaar** (**2**). Walk through the **Temple of the Town Gods** (**3**; p25), exiting the temple's north door onto Yuyuan Rd, and turn left. Keep walking west through the bazaar with the pond to your north (the road then becomes Bailing Rd). Turn right onto Old Jiaochang Rd, taking the first left to explore the gorgeous Buddhist **Chenxiangge Nunnery** (**4**; p22). Stroll to the end of Chenxiangge Rd, then turn left down Houjia Rd and take the first right into Zihua Rd. Diagonally north across Central Henan Rd at the end of Zihua Rd is Dajing Rd, a gritty portrait of low-slung houses and noodle restaurants. Near the end of the road on the right is the recently relocated **Baiyun Temple** (**5**; p22), separated from the **Dajing Pavilion** (**6**; p20) by Dajing Lane. Reaching Renmin Rd, head south and take the first right, walk to the end of Huiji Rd and then turn left onto South Xizang (Tibet) Rd. Explore the marvellous **Flower, Bird, Fish & Insect Market** (**7**) then cross the road into Liuhekou Rd – look out for the antiques stalls – and then take a left into the impressive **Dongtai Rd Antique Market** (**8**; p41). At the south end of Dongtai Rd turn right into the small alley, then down the first alley on the left and make your way south to Central Fuxing Rd, finishing up at the **Fazangjiang Temple** (**9**; p23).

Fear his wrath, Temple of the Town Gods

Distance 2.5km **Duration** 2hr
▶ **Start** Fuyou Antiques Market ● **End** Fazangjiang Temple

French Concession 法国租界

Commence your walk with a tour of **Xintiandi** (**1**; p17) and a visit to the **Site of the 1st National Congress of the Chinese Communist Party (CCP)** (**2**; p27) before heading west to walk through **Fuxing Park** (**3**; p31) and on to the Russian Orthodox **St Nicholas Church** (**4**), now housing a restaurant. Head back down Sinan Rd past the former residences of **Sun Yatsen** (**5**; p22) and **Zhou Enlai** (**6**; p22) before walking west along Central Fuxing Rd to wander through the grounds of the **Ruijin Guesthouse** (**7**; p73) and perhaps a fortifying drink at Face. On South Maoming Rd, bear north and cross Central Huaihai Rd to the **Okura Garden Hotel** (**8**; p72), originally the French Club. Visit the east wing for

Don't forget to say grace at St Nicholas

its splendid Art Deco features. Across South Maoming Rd rises the buildings of the **Jinjiang Hotel** (**9**; p72), including the smart Grosvenor House

Hengshan Moller Villa Hotel

in the south. Further north on the corner of Changle Rd and South Maoming Rd is the **Lyceum Theatre** (**10**; p66). Follow Changle Rd east to South Shaanxi Rd and north to the whimsical **Hengshan Moller Villa** (**11**; p20), where you can round off your walk with a snack and a coffee at the Bonomi Café.

Distance 4km **Duration** 4hr
▶ **Start** Ⓜ South Huangpi Rd ⏺ **End** Ⓜ Shimen No 1 Rd/Jing'an Temple

DAY TRIPS
Suzhou 苏州

If you enjoyed the Yuyuan Gardens in Shanghai's Old Town, Suzhou should top your excursions list. Famed for its classical Chinese gardens, Suzhou is similarly celebrated for its silk production and, apocryphally, for the prettiness of local women. Located on the Grand Canal – a waterway that once linked South China with Beijing – Suzhou is an occasionally picturesque canal town with more than its fair share of disfiguring and uninspiring white-tile buildings. Rent a bike for the day and take to Suzhou's streets.

The **Garden of the Master of the Nets** (off Shiquan Jie; Y15; ☯ 8am-5pm) is Suzhou's smallest garden, originally laid out in the 12th century and noted for its use of space. Many visitors admire the **Humble Administrator's Garden** (178 Dongbei Jie; Y32/16; ☯ 7.30am-

Garden of the Master of the Nets

5.30pm) and its crop of Ming dynasty features. Other gardens include **Garden For Lingering In** (79 Liuyuan Lu; Y30; ☯ 7.30am-5.30pm) and the **Blue Wave Pavilion** (off Renmin Lu; Y8; ☯ 8am-4.30pm).

The **Suzhou Silk Museum** (661 Renmin Lu; Y7; ☯ 9am-5.30pm) introduces visitors to the city's famed silk industry. Suzhou also has several notable temples and pagodas, including the nine-storey **North Temple Pagoda** (652 Renmin Lu; Y10; ☯ 7.30am-6pm), the Taoist **Temple of Mystery** (Guanqian Jie; Y10; ☯ 7.30am-5pm), which was originally founded in the 3rd century and notable for its vast Sanqing Hall, and the marvellous Buddhist **West Garden Temple** (Xiyuan Lu; Y10; ☯ 7.30am-5.30pm). Straddling the moat in the southwest of town, the **Pan Men area** (1 Dong Dajie; Y20; ☯ 8am-5pm) is worth visiting for surviving chunks of the city wall, views of **Wumen Bridge** and **Ruiguang Pagoda** (Y7), the oldest pagoda in Jiangsu province.

Hangzhou 杭州

One of China's premier tourist sights, Hangzhou is famed for its West Lake and scenic attractions. The city – a settlement has existed here since the Qin dynasty – has been spruced up over recent years and is now a clean, green and well-tended town, especially in the lakeside districts. Marco Polo breezed through Hangzhou in the 13th century, noting that it was one of the world's finest and most splendid cities. Many of its glories were tragically devastated during the Taiping Rebellion of the mid-19th century.

Hangzhou's focal point and picturesque hub is the **West Lake** with its gardens, bridges, pavilions and pagodas. Aim to see the lake at either dawn or dusk, which accentuate its charms. Connected to the northern shore by the long arm of the Baidi Causeway, the lake's largest island, **Gushan**, is the site of the **Zhejiang Provincial Museum** (Y15; ☉ 9am-4pm Tue-Sun & noon-4pm Mon) and **Zhongshan Park** (free). Boats also ferry tourists to **Xiaoying Island**, which to the south rise up small pagodas known as **Three Pools Mirroring the Moon**. You can clamber to the top of the huge **Leifeng Pagoda** (Y40; ☉ 8am-5.30pm) on the southern shore for superb views over the lake. South of the pagoda, the **China Silk Museum** (73-1 Yuhuangshan Lu; Y10; ☉ 8.30am-4pm) contains interesting displays. On the north side of Beishan Lu north of the lake is the **Temple of Yue Fei**, dedicated to the 12th-century patriot and general.

Hangzhou's most famous temple is the huge **Lingyin Temple** (Lingyin Lu; Y20; ☉ 7am-5pm), its main hall encapsulating a 20m-high camphorwood statue of Sakyamuni.

INFORMATION

170km southwest of Shanghai

- 🚆 fast trains depart Shanghai Train Station every hour or so for Hangzhou (2hr)
- 🚌 regularly from Shanghai's Hengfang Rd bus station & Xujiahui bus station; weekend tour buses from Shanghai Stadium (2½hr)
- 🚢 overnight Hangzhou–Suzhou boat along the Grand Canal departs daily at 5.30pm from jetty north of Huancheng Beilu; boats arrive in Suzhou at 7am. Departures from Suzhou are also at 5.30pm
- 🍽 Louwailou Restaurant (☎ 8796 9023; 30 Gushan Rd, on Gushan Island)

Apocalyptic sunset over West Lake

Shopping

Shanghai's most famous shopping street, East Nanjing Rd is served by toy trains that ferry shoppers laden with goods and tourists along its pedestrianised length. For souvenirs and knick-knacks, head to the Old Town, and take in Huaihai Rd in the French Concession for your smart shopping needs. Supersize malls favour Pudong, but the best malls and department stores can be found in Xujiahui, Huaihai Rd and Nanjing Rd. For shoes, shop at Shaanxi Rd, for books browse along Fuzhou Rd and for musical instruments, try Fenyang Rd and East Jinling Rd. Most shops are open daily from 10am to 9pm, though government-run stores often close at 6pm. Shopping malls and department stores are generally open till 10pm, especially on the weekends.

Still casting a watchful eye

Large tourist shops can generally arrange packing and postage. Payment for items in large stores (and pharmacists) can be old-fashioned; after you select a purchase, the sales assistant will give you a ticket which you take to the till *(shōuyíntái)*. After paying, you then retrace your steps to pick up your goods.

Is this how Mao envisioned his People's Republic?

DEPARTMENT STORES & MALLS

CITIC Square
中信泰富广场 (5, C5)
Covering six floors, this modern and top-end mall has a strong accent on top-end clothing and a generous spread of restaurants.
☎ 6218 0180 ✉ 1168 West Nanjing Rd ⏰ 10am-10pm Ⓜ Shimen No 1 Rd ♿ OK

Friendship Store
友谊商店 (5, J5)
It belongs to a vanishing era, but the Friendship Store plies useful souvenir items for the folks back home and last minute gift-shopping panic: jade, jewellery, antiques (fixed prices) and a decent selection of books.
☎ 6337 3555 ✉ 68 East Jinling Rd ⏰ 9.30am-9.30pm Ⓜ Middle Henan Rd

Grand Gateway
港汇广场 (8, B1)
With its glittering twin towers rising over Xujiahui metro station, the vast Ganghui mall has been dealt a strong hand in sports, toys, clothing and restaurants, with the

Paradise Cinema City on the 6th floor.
☎ 6407 0115 🖳 www .grand-gateway.com ✉ 1 Hongqiao Rd, Xujiahui ⏰ 10am-10pm Ⓜ Xujiahui ♿ OK

Superbrand Mall
正大广场 (6, B3)
The Thai-owned Superbrand is the city's most humungous mall. Virtually deserted midweek at midday, this also means the shops and restaurants can be crowd-free and the best time to visit. The Bonomi Café (p52) – and other restaurants in the building's western end – on the 5th floor offer stirring views of the Bund.
☎ 6887 7888 ✉ 168 Lujiazui Rd ⏰ 10am-10pm Ⓜ Lujiazui ♿ OK

Westgate Mall
梅陇镇伊势丹 (5, C5)
One of Shanghai's most popular malls for expat shoppers, the Westgate has a good basement supermarket and a wide range of smart clothing retailers.
☎ 6272 1111 ✉ 1038 West Nanjing Rd ⏰ 10am-10pm Ⓜ Shimen No 1 Rd ♿ OK

MARKETS

The Shanghai authorities regularly trot out banners in bad English condemning counterfeiting and the soliciting of customers, but it's all just hot air. The *páilóu* (gateway) at the western entrance to Xiangyang Market is inscribed with the characters '*yīkèwéizūn*', meaning 'put the customer first'. Taking this at face value, market hawkers are paparazzi-like in their attentions and fending them off can verge on the physical.

Dongjiadu Cloth Market
董家渡织品市场 (2, C2)
You won't get stitched up here, hands down the cheapest market for cloth in town. If you are hunting for cloth – wool, silk, cashmere – come here and if you need a custom-made outfit, several tailors can get you suited up.
✉ Dongjiadu Rd ⏰ 9am-5pm Ⓜ Middle Henan Rd ♿ poor

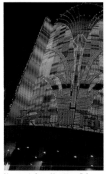
Neon nights, Nanjing Rd

HAGGLE
Haggling in markets is simply standard procedure. Come in at around 30% to 40% of the asking price, or lower if you think there's more slack to work with. Don't argue, keep smiling and simply walk away if you think the price is too high. Vendors at Xiangyang Market are used to foreigners paying well over the odds, so they will start off way too high. Vendors will typically punch a figure into a calculator, wave it in your face and then factor it down till you agree on a price. Compare prices at stalls and see how low vendors will go. Haggling is generally not possible at shops where prices are clearly marked.

FAKING IT

Like the rest of China, Shanghai is divided into two in-compatible realms: the official world and the real world. The official version has faked goods being swept off the streets, while even the most casual of glances on the street reveals a deluge of counterfeit goods. If goods are faked, then pay fake prices: at markets you can get up to 80% off the asking price so come in low. Scrutinise items carefully for tell-tale signs of shoddy workmanship – remember that bags fall apart, rucksacks split, jackets come asunder and Swiss Army penknives can disintegrate on their first encounter with a bottle of (fake?) Qingdao beer.

Dongtai Rd Antique Market
东台路古商品市场
(3, J2)
A short shuffle west of the Old Town perimeter, the Dongtai Rd Antique Market is a magnificent sprawl of curious, knick-knacks and Mao-era nostalgia. Roll up your sleeves, get set to rummage and hag-gle like there's no tomorrow.
✉ Dongtai Rd & Liuhekou Rd ⏰ 9am-6pm Ⓜ South Huangpi Rd ♿ poor

Fuyou Antique Market
福佑古玩市场 (4, B1)
Some finds still lurk among the junk, especially on Sunday mornings when things really start heaving.
✉ 457 Central Fangbang Rd ⏰ 9am-5pm Ⓜ Middle Henan Rd ♿ poor

Jingwen Flower Market
精文花市 (3, F4)
It may be shabby and sprawling, but this indoor flower market bursts with colour and fragrance, with an assortment of orchids, roses and creative bouquets.
✉ 225 South Shaanxi Rd ⏰ 8am-8pm Ⓜ South Shaanxi Rd ♿ poor

Temple of the Town Gods Market
城隍庙市场 (4, B1)
An unruly sprawl of curios, knick-knacks and knock-offs, this market really gets pumping weekends, when it overflows from the Huabao Building (265 Central Fang-bang Rd) into the Yuyuan Bazaar.
✉ Temple of the Town Gods, Central Fangbang Rd ⏰ 8.30am-9pm Ⓜ Middle Henan Rd ♿ poor

Xiangyang Market
襄阳市场 (3, E3)
Even if you wandered in here each arm sleeved in fake Rolexes, hawkers would still circle, baying 'Hel-loo, watchee'. Pitiful signs declare 'Maintain intellectual property', but that's before you get hit by the avalanche of fake Gucci, Polo, Burberry, Beckham football strip (pre-haggle Y280; post-haggle Y40) and DVDs. Haggle away, and if it all gets too much, beat a retreat to the veggie and fish market in the south of the market and eye up the blinking turtles and slither-ing creatures from the dark depths.
✉ cnr Central Huaihai Rd & Xiangyang Rd ⏰ 8am-9pm Ⓜ South Shaanxi Rd

Plenty of bargains to be snapped up at Xiangyang Market

CLOTHING & JEWELLERY

South Maoming Rd and Changle Rd are worth exploring for women's fashion and clothing boutiques.

Feel
金粉世家 (3, G4)
Opposite the Shanghai Art & Design Centre off Taikang Rd are these two small floors of traditional Chinese silk clothing and shoes for both men and women.
☎ 5465 4519 ✉ 2-21, Lane 210, Taikang Rd ⏰ 10am-7pm Ⓜ South Shaanxi Rd

Jooi Design (3, G4)
Upstairs in the Shanghai Art & Design Centre at the hub of the Taikang Rd Art Centre, Jooi's contemporary and imaginative designs have styled an eye-catching range of fashion accessories, lovely bags and home items.
✉ Studio 201-203, Shanghai Art & Design Centre, Lane 210, Taikang Rd ⏰ 10am-6pm Ⓜ South Shaanxi Rd

Shanghai Harvest Studio
上海盈稼坊工作室 (3, G4)
There's a dazzling collection of shoes, slippers, jackets, embroidery, hats and silver jewellery at this Taikang Rd Art Centre shop from the hands of Miao minority embroiderers on stools, hard at work. Embroidery classes (minimum four people) are also held here.
☎ 6473 4566 ✉ Shop 118, No 3 Bldg, Lane 210, Taikang Rd Ⓜ South Shaanxi Rd

Shanghai Tang
上海滩 (3, F2)
Bringing a vivacious rainbow splash to the west entrance of the Jinjiang Hotel, David Tang has brought his candy-coloured and frequently stunning clothing designs to the town that lent its name to his store. There's also a branch in Xintiandi.
☎ 5466 3006 🖥 www.shanghaitang.com ✉ 59 South Maoming Rd ⏰ 10am-10pm Ⓜ South Shaanxi Rd

Tantalising Shanghai Tang

Silk King
真丝大王 (5, H3)
One of Shanghai's largest silk outlets selling silk by the metre, silk clothes and custom-tailoring; several

CLOTHING & SHOE SIZES

Women's Clothing
Aust/UK	8	10	12	14	16	18
Europe	36	38	40	42	44	46
Japan	5	7	9	11	13	15
USA	6	8	10	12	14	16

Women's Shoes
Aust/USA	5	6	7	8	9	10
Europe	35	36	37	38	39	40
France only	35	36	38	39	40	42
Japan	22	23	24	25	26	27
UK	3½	4½	5½	6½	7½	8½

Men's Clothing
Aust	92	96	100	104	108	112
Europe	46	48	50	52	54	56

	S	M	M		L	
Japan						
UK/USA	35	36	37	38	39	40

Men's Shirts (Collar Sizes)
Aust/Japan	38	39	40	41	42	43
Europe	38	39	40	41	42	43
UK/USA	15	15½	16	16½	17	17½

Men's Shoes
Aust/UK	7	8	9	10	11	12
Europe	41	42	43	44½	46	47
Japan	26	27	27.5	28	29	30
USA	7½	8½	9½	10½	11½	12½

Measurements approximate only; try before you buy.

branches are dotted around town.
☎ 6321 2193 ✉ 66 East Nanjing Rd 🕓 9.30am-10pm Ⓜ Middle Henan Rd

Sunlight
桑澜 (3, G4)
This small specialist shop sells delicious piles of silk, cotton and cashmere scarves and shawls which make excellent presents.
☎ 6445 7516 🖳 www .wooscarf.com ✉ Shop 12, 7 Lane 210, Taikang Rd 🕓 9am-9pm Ⓜ South Shaanxi Rd

Traditional Chinese Clothes Salon
海上香侬 (3, F3)
South Maoming Rd has several shops where you can get tailor-made *(qípáo)* or off the peg. This small outfit just below the Art Deco Astrid Apartments has a splendid variety of silk dresses ranging from Y580 to Y1300.
☎ 6466 8441 ✉ 145 South Maoming Rd 🕓 10am-10pm Ⓜ South Shaanxi Rd

ARTS & CRAFTS

Liuligongfang
琉璃工坊 (8, B1)
Taiwan actress Yang Hui-han's dazzling and iridescent glass creations – exquisite objects radiating colour and lustre – range from earrings and necklaces to statues of Guanyin, Chinese *rúyì* sceptres and symbols of good fortune.
☎ 6407 0160 🖳 www .liuli.com ✉ Shop 127, 1st fl, Grand Gateway, 1 Hong-qiao Rd, Xujiahui 🕓 10am-10pm Ⓜ Xujiahui 🦽 good

Paspartout
七俗八土 (3, D3)
Blink and you'll miss it, this tiny nook-like place behind the red door is a treasure trove of Tibetan silver necklaces, ethnic bracelets, earrings, jackets, scarves, carvings, ornaments and decorations.
☎ 6248 3889 ✉ 106 Changhshu Rd 🕓 10am-10pm Ⓜ Changshu Rd

Skylight
天籁 (3, C4)
Sneak into this little incense-perfumed nook opposite the Embassy of Iran for its small haul of Tibetan handmade soap, silks, ethnic jewellery, antiques, Tibetan furniture (cabinet retailing at Y5200) and ethnic clothing. There may hardly be enough room

to turn around, but what's on offer is delightful.
☎ 6473 5610 ✉ 28 West Fuxing Rd 🕓 9.30am-9pm Ⓜ Changshu Rd

Spin
旋 (3, D2)
Jingdezhen ceramics with a trendy and modern spin, laid out in a concrete showroom set back from the road.
☎ 6279 2545 ✉ Bldg 3, 758 Julu Rd 🕓 noon-10pm Ⓜ Jing'an Temple/ Changshu Rd

Touche a Tour
异族情节 (3, F4)
Among the Southeast Asian handicrafts are some occasional finds, including Tintin written in Chinese (Y50).
☎ 6415 0301 ✉ 223 South Shaanxi Rd 🕓 10am-8pm Ⓜ South Shaanxi Rd

Tibetan wares at Skylight

Should be just enough here to scramble together to buy a beer, Dongtai Rd Antique Market

ANTIQUES

For details of Shanghai's antiques markets, see p40.

Art Deco
凹凸库家俱 (5, B2)
An elegant and smart shop on two floors selling Art Deco Shanghai furniture from the 1920s.
☎ 6277 8927 ⊠ Bldg 7, 50 Moganshan Rd ☺ 10am-7pm Ⓜ Shanghai Train Station

Dashanghai
大上海 (Map 2, C1)
While nosing around Duolun Rd (p25), pop into this shop for its deluge of Mao-era badges and propaganda posters, old records, photos, books, typewriters and an assortment of Shanghai

bric-a-brac from the days of decadence.
⊠ 181 Duolun Rd Ⓜ East Baoxing Rd light rail

Henry Antique Warehouse
亨利古典家具 (2, A3)
An excellent place to peruse for antique Chinese furniture with over 2000 pieces on display in a huge showroom, with English-speaking staff and packing and shipping all arranged.
☎ 6401 0831 ⌨ www.h-antique.com ⊠ 8 Hongzhong Rd (off Wuzhong Rd) ☺ 9am-6pm

Madame Mao's Dowry
毛太设计 (3, C4)
Two-floor modish outlet purveying Chinese retro chic, post-Liberation whatnots, furniture and ceramics, quality Cultural Revolution prints (Y200) and fashionable garments all under the beatific gaze of a weathered,

wooden Mao statue.
☎ 6437 1255 ⊠ 7 West Fuxing Rd ☺ 10am-7pm Ⓜ Hengshan Rd/ Changshu Rd

Shanghai Antique & Curio Store
上海古玩市场 (5, H4)
This state-run store is worth a rummage for its ceramics and jade. Haggling won't get you far, but most items have been approved and are authentic.
☎ 6321 4697 ⊠ 192-246 Guangdong Rd ☺ 9am-5pm Ⓜ Middle Henan Rd

Zhenjianzhai
甄鉴斋 (3, C3)
It's bedlam, but this cluttered and pokey jumble of old radios, furs, Buddhist statues, revolutionary knick-knacks, pipes, old irons and books still yields authentic and worthwhile finds among the dross.
☎ 5404 2024 ⊠ 98 Wuyuan Rd ☺ 9am-6pm Ⓜ Changshu Rd

MUSIC FOR THE MASSES
The good news is that Shanghai music CD shops (yīnxiàng diàn), often doubling as DVD retailers, are widespread. The bad news is that they all stock the same schlock. Judging by what fills the racks in Shanghai music stores, the high tidemark for Western music is the Eagles, the latest U2 album, Kenny G, Linkin Park, the Backstreet Boys and Mariah Carey. If you haven't already, now is the time to buy that MP3 player.

BOOKS

China National Publications Import-Export Corporation (CNPIEC) (5, C5)

It may be small, but this low-profile bookshop has a decent range of non-fiction. ☎ 5292 5214 ✉ 5th fl, CITIC Square, 1168 West Nanjing Rd ⏰ 10am-10pm Ⓜ Shimen No 1 Rd

Foreign Languages Bookstore

外文书店 (5, H4)
Plonk this bookshop on London's Charing Cross Rd and the bailiffs would be knocking within two weeks, but for the foreseeable future the 4th floor has the best selection of English language books in town, among the dated hardback dross and dust-collecting slabs of overstock. A smaller and quieter branch has set up shop diagonally across the way from Carrefour (where there is a single-room branch on the 2nd floor) in Gubei on Shuicheng Rd (Map 3, A3). ☎ 6322 3200 ✉ 390 Fuzhou Rd ⏰ 9.30am-6pm Sun-Thu, till 7pm Fri & Sat Ⓜ Middle Henan Rd

Garden Books

韬奋西文书局 (3, E2)
The ground floor can't work out whether it's a bookshop or an ice-cream parlour. With far more style (slate flagging, glass flooring) than substance (too much space, not enough books), there is, however, an impressive selection of literature in French upstairs, along with a so-so selection of books for tots. Copies of *International Herald*

TOME ALONE

Paris has its Shakespeare & Company, Kuala Lumpur's Skoob Books is a bibliophile's paradise and even Brussels can rustle up a Waterstone's, but when it comes to English language books, Shanghai is a basket case. For the country that invented paper and block printing (and in a city supporting a population of 100,000 expats), it's bewildering. When buying foreign titles, bookshops in Shanghai are forced to go through an import company which takes its own deep cut, making margins very slim indeed. You may stumble upon your quarry among the dust-collecting mounds of stale publications; otherwise finding a book in Shanghai is like fishing: you may not get what you want, but you'll take whatever turns up.

Tribune, *Time* and *Newsweek* are found at the till. ☎ 5404 8729/8728 ✉ 325 Changle Rd ⏰ 10am-10pm Ⓜ South Shaanxi Rd

Shanghai Museum Art Store

上海博物馆商店 (5, F5)
An excellent conclusion to a tour of the town's premier museum, visitors are greeted by heaps of books, Chinese arts and crafts, architecture, postcards and prints. Definitely worth a tour. ✉ 201 Renmin Ave ⏰ 9am-5pm Ⓜ Renmin Square/Renmin Park ♿ good

The communists' bible

FOOD & DRINK

Carrefour

家乐福 (7, A3)
This colossal *dàmàichǎng* (hypermarket) stocks all day-to-day essentials (including bicycles – which you can get licensed on the spot) and a well-stocked supermarket with expat rarities such as baked beans, Bovril and Vegemite. There's also a great food court, bakery and a useful free bus service round the back which has several lines to local locations. ☎ 6209 8899 ✉ 268 South Shuicheng Rd ⏰ 8am-10pm ♿ good

Cheese & Fizz

希利 (3, H2)
French gourmet delicatessen aimed at the affluent, international palates of Xintiandi: cured meats, wine, chilled-champagne, a select range of cheeses and on-site café. ☎ 6336 5823 ✉ Shop 105, 119 Madang Rd, North Block, Xintiandi ⏰ 9-1am Ⓜ South Huangpi Rd

City Supermarket
城市超市 (5, B5)

A fantastically stocked cornucopia of cured meats, cheeses, tinned foods, imported beers (Chimay, Newcastle Brown et al) and an excellent range of wines. Prices are steep but that hardly deters expat *taitais* (wives) from heaving overflowing baskets of delicacies and condiments to the till, heads lodged around mobiles. Other branches in town.

☎ 6279 8018 ✉ Shanghai Centre, 1376 West Nanjing Rd ☼ 8am-10.30pm Ⓜ Jing'an Temple/Shimen No 1 Rd

Gongdelin
功德林 (3, C3)

With a branch next door to their flagship restaurant, this vegetarian Chinese delicatessen sells a host of vegetarian tit-bits and they even sell their own brand of *mijiŭ* (rice wine; Y12 per bottle).

☎ 5403 9718 ✉ 249 Anfu Rd ☼ 6.30am-8pm Ⓜ Changshu Rd

Lianhua Supermarket
联华超市 (8, B1)

A fantastic store bountifully stocked with reasonably priced goods (plus there's a good deli).

☎ 6407 0115 ✉ Basement, Grand Gateway, 1 Hongqiao Rd, Xujiahui ☼ 10am-10pm Ⓜ Xujiahui ♿ good

FOR CHILDREN

Kids Village
宝贝城 (8, B1)

This large shop stocks a huge range of toys for all ages from the ubiquitous Ultraman, through to Spiderman, puzzles and gadgets.

☎ 6407 3461 ✉ 3rd fl, Grand Gateway, 1 Hongqiao Rd, Xujiahui ☼ 10am-10pm Ⓜ Xujiahui ♿ good

Tots – The Original Toy Store
原创玩具 (3, F3)

It may be small, but Tots has a decent range of toys and educational games.

☎ 5382 1106 ✉ 77 Ruijin No 2 Rd ☼ 10am-10pm Ⓜ South Shaanxi Rd

I tawt i taw a puddy tat. No wait, it's just a tourist

Good for scaring the kids

SPECIALIST STORES

Chinese Hand-painted Blue Nankeen Exhibition Hall
中国蓝印花布馆 (3, D3)

Buried down a meandering alley off Changle Rd, follow the signs to this shop, its courtyard hung with blue and white cloth. Perfect for gifts or keepsakes, the Jiangnan blue cotton (shoes, slippers, dresses, bedspreads and more) is patterned with traditional folk designs.

☎ 5403 7947 ✉ 24, Lane 637, Changle Rd ☼ 9am-5pm Ⓜ Changshu Rd

Golden Silk Road
波斯经典地毯 (5, B5)

Over two floors of an old house with polished floor boards, this smart shop has a tremendous range of Persian and Indian wool rugs (from Y2000). Good deals on Chinese silk rugs, made in Henan and Sichuan, can be found upstairs.

☎ 6289 2260 ✉ 1394 West Beijing Rd ☼ 10am-9pm Ⓜ Jing'an Temple

Huangshan Tea Company

黄山茶叶店 (2, F2)

The place to stock up on Huangshan *máofēng* or Hangzhou *lóngjǐng* tea leaves, as well as a host of other Chinese tea varieties.
☎ 5403 5412 ✉ 868 Central Huaihai Rd ☷ 10am-10pm Ⓜ South Shaanxi Rd

Torana House

图兰纳家苑 (3, E2)

Lovely place with handmade carpets and rugs made from Tibetan and Persian wool ranging from Y1000 to Y15,000. It also stages quite regular art and photographic exhibitions.
☎ 5404 7787 ▢ www .toranahouse.com ✉ 339-15 Changle Rd ☷ 10am-9pm Ⓜ South Shaanxi Rd

Yunhong Chopstick Shop

韵泓筷子商店 (5, H4)

Ideal for souvenir shopping or 11th hour gift buying, this slender shop on East Nanjing Rd is stuffed with Japanese and Chinese chopsticks of all decorative denominations: from bamboo, various woods, silver and gold-plated.
☎ 6322 0207 ✉ 387 East Nanjing Rd Ⓜ Middle Henan Rd

Offering a healthy dose of retail therapy, Nanjing Rd

ART GALLERIES

Also refer to the Sights and Activities chapter for reviews of other Shanghai art galleries that are sights in their own right (and some of which sell art works).

Mentaigne Gallery

蒙田画廊 (3, C3)

This charming French Concession gallery has regular exhibitions of contemporary Chinese art.
☎ 5404 3873 ✉ 149 Anfu Rd ☷ 10am-10pm Ⓜ Changshu Rd

New Red Door Gallery

新红门艺术 (3, G4)

This Taikang Rd Art Centre gallery has an excellent display of Chinese art works.

There is a further branch at 50 Moganshan Rd (p30).
☎ 6473 2593 ✉ No 5, Lane 220, Taikang Rd Ⓜ South Shaanxi Rd

Studio Rouge

红寨 (5, J4)

Up the steps a short shuffle east of the Captain Hostel, this trendy and smart gallery is hung with avant-garde Chinese art work and photographs in a well-lit space above a polished wooden floor.
☎ 6323 0833 ✉ 17 Fuzhou Rd ☷ 10.30am-6.30pm Ⓜ Middle Henan Rd

Wan Fung Art Gallery

云峰画廊 (8, B2)

In an exquisite setting on the ground floor of the former 19th-century Jesuit Library building (Bibliotheca Zi-Ka-Wei) (p15) in Xujiahui, the well-reputed Wan Fung Art Gallery has excellent Chinese paintings (oil paintings from Y15,000 to Y100,000), sculptures and prints (from Y80) for sale.
☎ 6487 4072 ext 107 ▢ www.wanfung.com.cn ✉ Bibliotheca Zi-Ka-Wei, 80 North Caoxi Rd ☷ 9.30am-7pm Ⓜ Xujiahui

SHANGHAI BY THE BOOK

From its decadent and revolutionary past to the narcissistic present, Shanghai has been eagerly chronicled by native and foreign scribes. For a traumatic insight into the Cultural Revolution, turn to Nien Cheng's memoir of the dark days in *Life and Death in Shanghai* (Penguin, 1988). The swinging Shanghai of yore is colourfully captured by Harriet Sergeant in her historical portrayal *Shanghai* (New York: Crown Publishers Inc, 1990).

Eating

After exploring the Bund, dining should top your menu of activities in Shanghai. An outgoing and inventive urban mentality constantly tests the boundaries of cooking, Shanghaiing top chefs from abroad and affixing the city to the world map of food with a glittering pin. Food fads come and go as regularly as the slew of booming vessels on the Huangpu River, circulating fresh ideas and dispatching yesterday's flavours to the bin. Swish restaurants open and close with metronome-like regularity, further keeping diners on their toes.

It's not just the dishes and utensils that make the Shanghai dining experience different from what you may be used to at home. To the Chinese, dining is first and foremost a social (and ostentatious) occasion, providing opportunities to cement *guānxì* (connections), rekindle friendships and seal business deals.

Rarely intimate spaces, large Chinese restaurants are often roomy, brightly lit and segmented by large round tables. Don't expect candlelight. If dinner for two is on your menu, you could find yourself perched at a cartwheel-sized table ringed by eight seats. Smart Chinese restaurants favour the full-on dining effect, so if you aim to cast a romantic spell over the evening, go international. Chinese waiting staff hover at the elbow while you peruse the menu, so tell them to vanish if you want time for your choice. At some Chinese restaurants, if you hang your coat on your chair, a sleeve is put over your jacket and the back of the chair. Tipping is not expected, however a service charge may be included in the bill.

MEAL COSTS

The pricing symbols used in this chapter indicate the cost for one person of a standard meal, excluding drinks.

$	under Y60
$$	Y60-140
$$$	Y141-300
$$$$	over Y300

Apart from Pudong and Xintiandi, a pleasantly socialist egalitarianism exists in restaurant locales. From a food perspective, central Shanghai has yet to be carved into exclusive/nonexclusive enclaves, so the shabbiest of hole-in-the-wall *jiǎozi* dens still cooks up across from the latest modern restaurant.

Urban jungle views from Kathleen's 5, West Nanjing Rd

THE BUND AND EAST NANJING RD

Over recent years, the Bund has attracted a host of elegant and smart international and Chinese restaurants aiming to capitalise on the waterfront's architectural exclusivity and classic panoramas. Restaurants further spill on down Nanjing Rd and parallel roads west to Renmin Square.

Ajisen Ramen
味千拉面 (5, H4)
Japanese Noodles $
Simply hopping come meal time, this Japanese noodle chain escorts diners to the noodle dish of their choice via easy-to-use photo menus and the assistance of diligent squads of staff in regulation black T-shirt and jeans. Go for the Kimuchi Dumpling in hot pot (Y23) – a steaming, chilli-infused blast of chunky dumplings, spicy cabbage and *jīnzhēn* mushrooms – guaranteed to bring out a sweat.
☎ 6360 7194 ✉ 327 East Nanjing Rd ⏰ 10am-10.30pm Ⓜ Middle Henan Rd

Jean Georges
让乔治 (5, J4)
French $$$$
One of the pillars of the ultrachic consortium Three on the Bund, Jean Georges complements their modern take on French cuisine with a simply gorgeous dining environment.
☎ 6321 7733 ✉ 4th fl, Three on the Bund, 3 First East Zhongshan Rd ⏰ 11.30am-2.30pm &

TOP ROMANTIC SPOTS
The food can be excellent, but ever-present waiting staff and the blinding lights of many Chinese restaurants can kill off a romantic soirée before the first drink arrives. **M on the Bund** (below) conjures up just the right balance of choice setting and intimacy, while an *escargot's* throw away, **Jean Georges** (below) casts just the right sort of romantic magic over dinner. East of the river, **Danieli's** (p56) delivers delicious nocturnal window-side views over to twinkling Lujiazui.

5.30-10.30pm Ⓜ Middle Henan Rd

Kathleen's 5 (5, E5)
European/Mediterranean $$-$$$
A classy production from Kathleen Lau, an old hand on the China bar scene. This roof-top restaurant/bar comes with indulgent views over Renmin Square – plus al fresco dining – from the top of the Shanghai Art Museum.
☎ 6327 2221 ✉ www.kathleens5.com.cn ✉ 5th fl, Shanghai Art Museum, 325 West Nanjing Rd ⏰ 11.30am-11.30pm Ⓜ Renmin Park/Renmin Square

M on the Bund
米氏西餐厅 (5, J4)
Continental $$$$
Table linen flapping in the breeze alongside exclusive roof-top views to Pudong, M on the Bund's elegant formula still elicits applause from Shanghai's foodies. Park yourself in a wicker chair, reach for the mismatched bone-handled cutlery and treat yourself to two-/three-course (Y118/138) set lunches or go the whole hog on the crispy suckling pig (Y198).
☎ 6350 9988 ✉ www.m-onthebund.com ✉ 7th fl, 20 Guangdong Rd ⏰ 11.30am-2.30pm & 6.15-10.30pm Ⓜ Middle Henan Rd

Number 5
外滩5号 (5, J4)
Western food $$
With excellent value scrummy set lunches (11am–2pm), this stylish basement Bund restaurant/bar is perfect for casual, comfy dining. Come evening, neck a brain haemorrhage, sip a slippery nipple (both Y30), seize a pool cue and tune into late night live jazz sounds. Has wireless Internet access.
☎ 6329 4558 ✉ www.numberfive.cn ✉ No 5 the Bund, First East Zhongshan Rd ⏰ 10am-2am Mon-Sat Ⓜ Middle Henan Rd

Prego 帕戈 (5, H4)
Italian $$-$$$
Modern and stylish without being overly chic, the Westin Shanghai's Italian restaurant is a smart – perhaps not romantic – option with a wood-fired pizza oven and open kitchen. ☎ 6335 1786 ✉ 2nd fl, Westin Shanghai, Bund Centre, 88 Central Henan Rd ⏲ 11am-11pm Ⓜ Middle Henan Rd

Ruzzi
如滋 (5, G4)
Italian $-$$
With pizzas as crisp and fresh as the layout, this chain is a slick operation. Park yourself on one of the comfy sofas, navigate the user-friendly menu and go for the Huff and Puff chowder soup (Y22), the excellent barbeque chicken pizza (Y43) and the Classic banana split (Y19). ☎ 6360 9031 ✉ 528 Fuzhou Rd ⏲ 11am-10pm Sun-Thu, 11am-11pm Fri & Sat Ⓜ Renmin Square

The Stage
舞台餐厅 (5, H4)
International $$$
Consistently voted in as Shanghai's most popular brunch spot, this ground floor restaurant in the top-notch Westin Shanghai sees long lines of devotees (especially for the seafood), so book ahead. Vegetarian options available. ☎ 6335 0577 ✉ The Bund Centre, 88 Central Henan Rd ⏲ 11.30am-3pm Ⓜ Middle Henan Rd

Wang Baohe Restaurant
王宝和 (5, G4)
Seafood $$$-$$$$
Connoisseurs of crustacean cuisine gather here –

originally dating from 1744 – to savour the soft flesh of crabs from Yangcheng Lake in Jiangsu province. The restaurant has a tight claw hold on the tourist circuit, so reservations are recommended. ☎ 6322 3673 ✉ 603 Fuzhou Rd ⏲ 11am-1pm & 5-8.30pm Ⓜ Renmin Square/Renmin Park

Whampoa Club
黄浦会 (5, J4)
Shanghainese $$$
This extraordinarily elegant restaurant with gorgeous Art Deco flourishes should be top of your list if you aim to dine at the exclusive pinnacle of Shanghai cuisine. ☎ 6321 3737 ✉ 5th fl, Three on the Bund ⏲ 11.30am-2.30pm & 5.30-10pm Ⓜ Middle Henan Rd

---

> ### ROOM WITH A VIEW
> Not all of Shanghai's restaurants open onto dust-choked streetscapes of honking taxis and white-tile apartment blocks streaked with rust. If you want more to seduce you than a fake Chen Yifei hanging over a refrigerator-sized air conditioning unit, book at a table at one of the following. **M on the Bund** (p49): the grand dame of extravagant al fresco views, with a lavish menu to boot. With views over Renmin Park, the rooftop **Kathleen's 5** (p49) gives you something else to savour, while **Lan Na Thai's** popular menu (p54) is accompanied by some choice vistas.

OLD TOWN

The Old Town is famed more for its traditional and chaotic hole-in-the-wall restaurants rather than sophisticated dining, but this means you can find all kinds of snacks being fried-up down alleyways and off main roads.

Huxinting Teahouse
湖心亭茶馆 (4, B1)
Tea house $
Get here early in the day for a window seat in this historic tea house (Y20 for green tea), ensconced in the middle of the Yuyuan Bazaar pond. ☎ 6373 6950 ✉ Jiuqu Bridge, Yuyuan Bazaar ⏲ 8.30am-10pm Ⓜ Middle Henan Rd

Contemporary art deco interior of the Whampoa Club

Nanxiang Steamed Bun Restaurant

南翔馒头店 (4, B1)
Dumplings $-$$

Tie in your trip to the Yuyuan Gardens with a sampling of mouth-watering pork, crab-meat or crab roe *xiǎolóngbāo* (steamed dumplings) at this celebrated restaurant (branches have opened abroad), compellingly advertised by patient queues out front. Takeaways are downstairs, while upstairs seating has views over the Mid-Lake Pavilion Teahouse.
☎ 6355 4206 ⊠ 378 Fuyou Rd, Yuyuan Bazaar ☻ 7am-8pm Ⓜ Middle Henan Rd

Steamed bun take away

HONGQIAO & GUBEI

Their dearth of sights and bars compounded by un-developed transport links means that few travellers delve into Hongqiao or Gubei. Hongqiao in par-ticular is sidelined and neg-lected, although Gubei has more of a profile as a popular expat residential area. The area has several restaurants of note that warrant a trip.

1221 (3, A4)

Shanghainese $$

This simple Shanghai restaur-ant rewards its loyal diners with an excellent value menu (in English) and commend-able service.
☎ 6213 6585 ⊠ 1221 West Yan'an Rd
☻ 11.30am-2pm & 5-11pm
Ⓜ Jiangsu Rd

Megabite

大食代 (7, A3)
Chinese/Asian $

If you're short of a calorie or two to tackle Carrefour, this high-grade ground floor food hall is the perfect pit stop. Purchase a card with credit points and choose from the huge selection of dishes to be cooked up on the spot.
⊠ 1st fl, Carrefour, 268 South Shuicheng Rd, Gubei; further branches around town including Raffles City (Map 5, F4) ☻ 8am-10pm

Dongbeiren

东北人 (3, A4)
Northeast Chinese $

The dumplings *(jiǎozi)* at this sprightly outfit are as true to the Chinese northeast as the gaggle of rouge-cheeked, pigtailed *Dōngběi* (northeast) waitresses. Besides tummy-filling lamb, pork and beef dumplings (Y10–16), aim for the tender Sun Island Flaming Dragon Fish (Y48) or the hefty boneless pork knuckle (Y48), but pass on the dry lamb kebabs.
☎ 5230 2230 ⊠ 46 Panyu Rd ☻ 11am-10pm
Ⓜ Zhongshan Park

Frankie's Place

兰奇餐厅 (2, A3)
Singaporean $$

Old-timer Frankie's has jumped around a bit over the years, largely taking his expat clientele with him, and is cur-rently taking root in the far-flung west end of Wuzhong Rd. Weekday set lunches are popular, with dishes includ-ing *laksa*, *nasi lemak* and *rojak* (Malay salads).
☎ 5476 1068 ⊠ 546 Huanghua Rd ☻ 9.30am-11pm

Moon River Diner

月亮河 (2, A3)
American $-$$

Located along the Hongmei Rd Food Street, the American

SNACKING IN SHANGHAI

You may not join the locals queuing at the *chòu dòufu* (smelly doufu) stall, but Shanghai's back alleys are stuffed with eats and treats. Start the day with a deep-fried dough stick *(yóutiáo)* and for lunch, hunt down a bowl of *málà tàng* – spicy soup into which you immerse skewer-loads of *dòufu* and vegetables – or settle for a steaming bowl of Muslim *lāmiàn* (noodles sprinkled with shreds of lamb) for lunch. Roadside lamb kebabs *(yángròuchuàn)* are a must – Kazakh and Uighur chefs from Xinjiang are the true masters. Sweet bubble tea *(nǎichá)* is both a thirst quencher and a snack in its own right – coming hot *(rè)* or iced *(bīngde)*.

BEST OF THE BRUNCH

Typically clocking in at brunch time, dim sum is a perfect brunch option, with **Crystal Jade Restaurant** (opposite) being one of the best in town for this Hong Kong snack. Yuyuan Garden brunchers gather at the excellent **Nanxiang Steamed Bun Restaurant** (p51). For Western brunch, the **Stage** (p50) at the **Westin Shanghai** (p70) routinely garners votes for its grade-A brunch and **Mesa** (p54) brings you excellent brunch in a charming French Concession context.

1950s-style Moon River Diner slides platefuls of excellent value burgers and huge all-day breakfasts under the noses of wide-eyed and nostalgia-tripping diners.
☎ 6465 8879 ✉ 17 Hongmei Rd Food Street, Lane 3338 Hongmei Rd
🕑 8am-10pm

THE FRENCH CONCESSION

With its Gallic pretensions, villa-style architecture and tree-lined streets, it is hardly surprising that the French Concession takes dining particularly seriously. Xintiandi attracts Chinese and expat diners to its stylish array of eateries, while an eclectic range of world cuisine characterises the rest of the district, meaning most of your food needs can be met here.

Art Salon
艺术沙龙 (3, G2)
Shanghainese $-$$
Excellent Shanghai dishes served in bohemian surroundings with giant, high-backed chairs and walls decked out with paintings

Art Salon restaurant

(the work of one of the two proprietor brothers). After your meal, tuck as much furniture, art and whatnots as you can under your arm (it's all for sale).
☎ 5306 5462 ✉ 164 Nanchang Rd 🕑 10.30am-10pm
Ⓜ South Shaanxi Rd

Ashanti Dome
阿香蒂 (3, G3)
French $$$-$$$$
With an unrivalled setting within the St Nicholas Russian Orthodox Church on pretty Gaolan Rd, this is one of Shanghai's most popular restaurants, so reservations are essential. Boca, a tapas bar, is also located here.
☎ 5306 6777 ✉ 16 Gaolan Rd Ⓜ South Huangpi Rd
🕑 6pm-midnight Sun & Mon, 6pm-1am Tue-Sat

Baoluo Jiulou
保罗酒楼 (3, D2)
Shanghainese $-$$
It may seem a tad pokey in parts, but Baoluo is big on flavour, low on cost and draws many a fickle Shanghai diner – open all through the night and wee hours.
☎ 5403 7239 ✉ 271 Fumin Rd 🕑 11am-6am
Ⓜ Changshu Rd

Boduo Xinji
博多新记 (3, E3)
Cantonese/Chaozhou $
Just glance through the window of this cramped outpost of Cantonese/Chaozhou cuisine and note the ease with which it takes Shanghai's notoriously fickle diners hostage with a much loved, spot on menu. Three branches in town.
☎ 5404 9878 ✉ 9 Xinle Rd
🕑 11am-2pm & 5-10.30pm
Ⓜ South Shaanxi Rd/Changshu Rd

Bonomi Café
波纳米 (3, E1)
Café $-$$
Park yourself next to the lawn of the fairytale Hengshan Moller Villa for a long, leisurely taste of Shanghai's most superbly located café. It simply doesn't get better than this, so supersize your cappuccino and unwind.
☎ 6247 5003 ✉ Hengshan Moller Villa, 30 South Shaanxi Rd 🕑 10am-midnight Ⓜ Shimen No 1 Rd/Jing'an Temple/South Shaanxi Rd

Boonna Café
布那咖啡 (3, E2)
Café $
The quiet, introspective Boonna is set back from the

action next to Boduo Xinji (opposite) on leafy Xinle Rd. Try the excellent house coffee (Y10) and banana pancakes (Y20). Guests get 30-minutes free use of Internet.

☎ 5404 6676 ✉ 88 Xinle Rd ⏰ 9am-1am Ⓜ South Shaanxi Rd/Changshu Rd

Café Montmartre
梦曼特 (3, E3)
French $-$$
Bumping into this clever imitation of a Latin Quarter brasserie perched next to noisy Xiangyang Market is like running into an old Parisian friend, wreathed in the aroma of Ricard and Gaulloise fumes. There is a bar and café tables below, as well as upstairs seating and outside terrace. Set lunches (Y48) include the filling salmon *rillettes*.

☎ 5404 7658 ✉ 55 South Xiangyang Rd ⏰ 11am-midnight Ⓜ South Shaanxi Rd/Changshu Rd

Crystal Jade Restaurant
翡翠酒家 (3, H2)
Cantonese/Shanghainese $$
Justifiably popular for its affordable and delicious Hong Kong dim sum and *lamian*

(hand pulled noodles), this Xintiandi branch of the Singaporean chain is often full, so make reservations well ahead.

☎ 6385 8752 ✉ 2nd fl, Unit 12A & B, House 6-7, South Block, Lane 123, Xinye Rd, Xintiandi ⏰ 11am-3pm & 5-11.30pm Mon-Fri, 10.30am-3pm & 5-11.30pm Sat & Sun Ⓜ South Huangpi Rd

Dishuidong
滴水洞 (3, F2)
Hunan $-$$
Its name literally meaning Dripping Water Cave, this inconspicuous and simple top-floor Hunan restaurant, staffed by waitresses in pretty Hunan blue cloth, is easily missed on a wander down South Maoming Rd. The Mao Gong braised pork (Y28) – a plate of large lumps of fatty pork in a mild soup-sauce – makes for chunky mouthfuls and the *mála dòufǔ* – a sweltering bowl of *dòufǔ* in a fire-red sauce – is a sure fire scorcher. Several branches in town.

☎ 6253 2689 ✉ 2nd fl, 56 South Maoming Rd ⏰ 9.30-2am Ⓜ South Shaanxi Rd

G-Sushi
元绿寿司 (3, H2)
Japanese $$
A creation of *gōngfu* maestro Dr Jacky Chan, the modern G-Sushi delivers enjoyable doses of style and good-value lunch sets in a spacious and well-designed venue.

☎ 6335 3395 ✉ 202, 2nd fl, Hong Kong New World Plaza, 300 Central Huaihai Rd ⏰ 11.30am-2pm & 5-10pm Ⓜ South Huangpi Rd

Guyi Hunan Restaurant
古意 (3, D2)
Hunan $$
You may need to aim for a seat directly under the air-conditioner at this spicy, chilli-infused restaurant that does palate-blistering recipes from Hunan.

☎ 6249 5628 ✉ 1st fl, Jufu Bldg, 87 Fumin Rd ⏰ 11.30am-2pm & 5.30-10.30pm Ⓜ Jing'an Temple

Herbal Legend
百草传奇 (3, H2)
Chinese $$-$$$
If you require a curative repast, need to balance your *yīn* and *yáng* or are simply driven by curiosity, this Xintiandi restaurant blends

FOOD STREETS
Shanghai's bustling food streets – jam-packed with snack stalls and jostling with diners eating on the move – have dwindled on the back of galloping development and more demanding palates. The handful of central food streets resisting the times include Huanghe Rd north of Renmin Square, which remains a favourite for noodles and *ròuchuàn* (kebabs). The section of Yunnan Rd linking East Yan'an Rd and East Jinling Rd is a further bustling strip of vocal kebab-sellers and snacks. For a full-on array of local snacks, trawl Wujiang Rd (Map 5, D5) running south of West Nanjing Rd and divided by Shimen No 1 Rd.

XIAOLONGBAO 小笼包

Xiǎolóngbāo – steamed dumplings – are to Shanghai what *dim sum* are to Hong Kong. Shanghai's tastiest snacks, *xiǎolóngbāo* can be found everywhere. Cooked in bamboo steamers *(lóng)*, these bite-sized, meat-filled morsels also contain scalding meat juice, so don't down them in one but instead take exploratory nibbles or split it open first and let the boiling broth escape

Chinese medicinal preparations into all its tasty and restorative dishes and soups.
☎ 6386 6817 ✉ House 1, South Block, Lane 123, Xinye Rd, Xintiandi ⏲ 11am-1am Ⓜ South Huangpi Rd

KABB
凯搏西餐厅 (3, H2)
American $$
KABB's outside seating, perfect Xintiandi location and winning bar brings an extra dimension to its filling menu of whole-hearted American/ Mexican and Italian hits – burgers, Tex-Mex, club sandwiches and pasta.
☎ 3307 0798 ✉ 5 North Block, Lane 181, Taicang Rd, Xintiandi ⏲ 6.30am-late Ⓜ South Huangpi Rd

Kaveen's Kitchen
正宗印度菜 (3, C2)
Indian $-$$
Above the Old Manhattan Bar, Kaveen's – official caterer for Air India flights out of town – is a well-liked spot on Shanghai's cluttered food map. It's a bit cramped (the owner moved here from Kowloon, so perhaps he doesn't notice) but the menu has room for most tastes, including vegetarian. Try the excellent *Aloo Palak* (spinach and potato) with some naan.
☎ 6248 8292 ✉ 2nd fl, 231 Huashan Rd ⏲ 11.30am-

2.30pm & 5.30pm-1am Ⓜ Jing'an Temple

Kommune
公社酒吧 (3, G4)
Café $
A trendy spot for a coffee in the Taikang Rd Arts Centre, with aluminium furniture and Y48 Sunday big breakfasts.
☎ 6466 2416 ✉ No 7, Lane 210, Taikang Rd ⏲ 10am-7pm

Lan Na Thai
兰纳泰 (3, G3)
Thai $$$
Ease into low gear sinking a drink at Face Bar (p61) before strolling upstairs to take a seat amid the delicious décor of this (admittedly pricey) landmark Thai restaurant, with choice views attached.
☎ 6466 4328 ✉ Bldg 4, Ruijin Guesthouse, 118 Ruijin No 2 Rd ⏲ noon-2.30pm & 5.30-10.30pm Ⓜ South Shaanxi Rd

Mesa (3, D2)
Continental $$$
All space and light, Mesa's impressive continental menu works its magic best after apéritifs at its adjacent bar, Manifesto. In warm weather, the voluminous interior spills out onto the terrace decking above Julu Rd.
☎ 6289 9108 ✉ 748 Julu Rd ⏲ 11.30am-2.30pm

& 6-11pm, brunch 10am-5pm Sat & Sun Ⓜ Jing'an Temple/Changshu Rd ♿

Marco Polo
马哥孛罗面包 (3, G2)
Bakery $
With branches all over Shanghai, Marco Polo is an excellent source of fresh bread, cakes and pastry snacks.
☎ 5306 3867 🖥 www .marco-polo.cn ✉ 632 Central Huaihai Rd ⏲ 8am-10pm Ⓜ South Shaanxi Rd/South Huangpi Rd

Nepali Kitchen
尼泊尔餐厅 (3, D2)
Nepalese $-$$
Arranged delightfully over 4 floors, take your pick from the larger seating areas or the small rooms tucked away and strewn with cushions.
☎ 5404 6281 ✉ 4, Lane 819, Julu Rd ⏲ 11.30-2pm & 6-11pm Tue-Sun, 6-11pm Mon Ⓜ Jing'an Temple/ Changshu Rd

Old China Hand Reading Room
汉源书室 (3, F4)
Café $
If Starbucks is finally getting up your nostrils, sample the more refined aroma of this coffee house, decorated with old books and images of old Shanghai, courtesy of café

patron and photographer Deke Erh.

☎ 6473 2526 ✉ 27 Shaoxing Rd ☾ 10am-midnight Ⓜ South Shaanxi Rd

People on the Water

水上人家 (3, C2)

Ningbo $$$

Stroll downstairs to this sleek, new Ningbo restaurant, to be greeted by a fish tank glittering with golden *fācáiyú* (literally 'get rich fish'), a prelude to the fine coastal Zhejiang seafood to follow. With over 150 dishes on view, menus are dispensed with, making ordering a breeze.

☎ 6248 0000 ext 1830 ✉ Basement, Hilton Hotel, 250 Huashan Rd ☾ 11.30am-2.30pm & 5.30-10.30pm Ⓜ Jing'an Temple

Quanjude

全聚德 (3, F2)

Peking Duck $$

Purists may scoff that true Peking Duck has to be consumed within earshot of the Forbidden City, but this celebrated eatery from the capital is a particularly appetizing plan B. Three branches around town.

☎ 5404 5799 ▱ www .shanghaiquanjude.com ✉ 4th fl, 786 Central Huaihai Rd ☾ 11am-11pm Ⓜ South Shaanxi Rd

Shikumen Bistro

法蓝极榀 (3, H2)

French-Mediterranean $$$

Much-acclaimed platters from chef Jean Alberti lure impressed expat French crowds to this tasteful and elegant Xintiandi restaurant and bar. Get a look in on the culinary action at the open kitchen, or mosey upstairs to the cigar lounge and rare wines room.

☎ 6386 7100 ▱ www .shikumenbistro.com ✉ 5 North Block, Lane 181, Taicang Rd, Xintiandi ☾ 11am-2.30pm & 5.30pm-12.30am Ⓜ South Huangpi Rd

Shintori

新都里无二店 (3, D2)

Japanese $$$

The bamboo-lined approach does little to prepare diners for the setting of this Japanese restaurant, trendily poised somewhere between a Wehrmacht bunker and a Brutalist penal institution. Straight edges, sharp lines, cold concrete, open kitchen: read cerebral dining.

☎ 5404 5252 ✉ 803 Julu Rd Ⓜ Jing'an Temple/Changshu Rd

Taco Popo

墨西哥快餐店 (5, B6)

Mexican $

An excellent value stomach filling for those on the Tongren Rd bar run or in need of some serious Mexican snacking: burritos, nachos and enchiladas, laced with but a hint of spice.

☎ 6289 3602 ✉ 78-80 Tongren Rd ☾ 11am-4am Ⓜ Jing'an Temple

T8 Restaurant & Bar

T8餐厅 (3, H2)

Continental/Fusion $$$$

At the lofty apex of Shanghai dining, T8's concoctions takes diners to new levels of flavour and irresistibility, in an ultra-stylish dining environment geared around its Mediterranean menu and lively open kitchen. T8's brunches attract crowds of faithful returnees.

☎ 6355 8999 ✉ 8 North Block, Lane 181, Taicang Rd, Xintiandi ☾ 11am-1pm & 6pm-1am (closed lunch Tue) Ⓜ South Huangpi Rd

T8 Restaurant & Bar

CAFÉ CULTURE

To its glut of hit-and-miss bars, Shanghai adds a surplus of ho-hum cafés. Forgo the rest and follow your caffeine cravings to **Bonomi Café** (p52), an excellent chain that has staked claim to prime chunks of real estate – in the HSBC Building on the Bund, across the water with a fine view of the Bund in the Superbrand Mall and lawn-side at the dreamy Hengshan Moller Villa. Tune out from Shanghai's hectic vibe at **Boonna Café** (p52). Arranged over three floors of a gorgeous old villa, enjoy a brew at the **Old Film Café** (p58), overlooked by stills of Audrey Hepburn, Marilyn Monroe, Humphrey Bogart and Vivien Leigh.

VEGETARIAN PICKS

As a moral or health concern, vegetarianism is not big in carnivorous Shanghai and is largely the preserve of conscientious Buddhists. If you eschew all meat, ordering vegetable dishes from standard restaurants may not guarantee a flesh-free meal (meat stock could be used), but if you want to be sure what's pinched between your chopsticks, dine at the following. The elegantly refurbished Buddhist **Gongdelin** (opposite; pictured below) delivers a fine fleshless menu in a civilised ambience with spiritual overtones. Avoid accidentally ordering phoenix claws or duck's neck at **Zaozishu** (right).

Gongdelin comes as a welcoming relief for vegetarians

Va Bene
华万意 (3, H2)
Italian $$$
Book ahead for a table at this civilised, 2-floor Italian corner in Xintiandi, to savour choice mouthfuls from its celebrated antipasto, *zuppa*, pasta, pizza, pesce and *carne* menu, rounded off with some delectable *dolce*. The *linguine alle vongole veraci* (linguine with clams, garlic and olive oil) hits the spot.
☎ 6311 2211 ⌨ www .vabeneshanghai.com ✉ 7 North Block, Lane 181, Taicang Rd, Xintiandi Ⓜ South Huangpi Rd

Wuyue Renjia
吴越人家 (3, F2)
Noodles $
Stuffed away down an alley off Huaihai Rd, this pocket-sized noodle house is the best thing since sliced bread. The calming traditional Chinese décor is perfectly complemented by steaming bowls of wholesome noodles. You may have to share your table with a stranger or two and decode the Chinese menu, but our advice is to go for the *yúxiāng ròusīmiàn* (Y13) and the fine bite-sized chunks of *cōngyóutāng húntun* (Y6).
☎ 5306 5410 ✉ No 10, Alley 706, Central Huaihai Rd ⏰ 10.30am-3pm & 4.30-9pm Ⓜ South Shaanxi Rd

Xiao Nan Guo
小南国 (3, G3)
Shanghainese $$$
The Ruijin Guesthouse branch of Xiao Nan Guo is the archetypal big Chinese dining experience – a glaring, floodlit and cavernous dining space – with deservedly famous food.
☎ 6466 2277 ✉ 2nd fl, Ruijin Guesthouse, 118 Ruijin No 2 Rd ⏰ 11am-2pm & 5-9.30pm Ⓜ South Shaanxi Rd

Zaozishu 枣子树 (3, H1)
Chinese Vegetarian $$
With two branches in town, Zaozishu is one of Shanghai's most popular vegetarian restaurants.
☎ 6384 8000 ✉ 77 Songshan Rd ⏰ 10am-9pm Ⓜ South Huangpi Rd

Zentral Healthy Eatery
膳趣健康膳食 (3, J3)
Salads & Sandwiches $
Clamber out of the MSG sea and come here for affordable lunch sets, crispy and tasty healthy salads and sandwiches. Zentral's low on the oil but high on taste and appeal. There's another branch in Pudong.
☎ 6374 5815 ⌨ www .zentral.com.cn ✉ 567 South Huangpi Rd ⏰ 10am-10pm Ⓜ South Huangpi Rd

PUDONG

Mention Pudong and watch Shanghai diners choke on their noodles. The architecture may be in the clouds, but decent Pudong dining options are limited to international hotels and shopping malls.

Danieli's
Italian $$$
The dining desert of Pudong has the occasional oasis and it comes as little surprise

that the St Regis provides some of the Italian cuisine in Shanghai. Cleaved in two by the building's twin leaves, there's a busy open kitchen, a warm interior, long views and a regularly changing menu.
☎ 5050 4567 ✉ 29th fl, the St Regis, 889 Dongfang Rd ⏰ 11.30-2.30pm, 6-11pm Tue-Fri & 6-11pm Sat Ⓜ Dongfang Rd

WEST NANJING RD AND JING'AN

Bali Laguna
巴厘岛 (3, D2)
Indonesian $$$
Superbly located lakeside in Jing'an Park, this popular Indonesian restaurant is gorgeously presented with dark wood décor and overseen by elegant waiting staff in sarongs. Bar attached.
☎ 6248 6970 ✉ 189 Huashan Rd ⏰ 11am-2.30pm & 6-10.30pm Ⓜ Jing'an Temple

Bandu Cabin
半度雨棚 (5, B2)
Café $
Elude the crowds at this quiet, civilised and music-oriented café while art-watching at 50 Moganshan Rd (p30) west of Suzhou Creek. Bandu produce music and a range of CDs (largely classical Chinese music) is on display; at the time of writing classical Chinese music performances were being staged, but phone ahead for the latest.
☎ 6276 8267 🖳 www .bandumusic.com ✉ Bldg No 11, 50 Moganshan Rd ⏰ 10am-6.30pm Ⓜ Shanghai Train Station

Bi Feng Tang
避风塘 (5, B6)
Cantonese $$
With five branches around Shanghai – including a 24-hour branch at 175 Changle Rd – Bi Feng Tang's success builds on its affordable Cantonese dim sum snacks lapped up by a loyal local and expat fan base. English menu.
☎ 6279 0738 ✉ 1333 West Nanjing Rd ⏰ 9.30am-5am Ⓜ Jing'an Temple

Element Fresh (5, B5)
Sandwiches $$
With an emphasis on fresh and crisp ingredients, this swish sandwich parlour is a must for vegetarians and non-veggies alike.
☎ 6279 8682 ✉ Room 112, Shanghai Centre, 1376 West Nanjing Rd ⏰ 7am-11pm Mon-Thu & Sun, 7am-midnight Fri & Sat Ⓜ Jing'an Temple

Gongdelin
功德林 (5, E5)
Chinese Vegetarian $-$$
The podgy effigy of Milefo and the faint aroma of temple incense hint at the Bud-

dhist creed of this elegantly refitted vegetarian restaurant, housed in a red-brick building dating from 1922. The fleshless food – served in a graceful environment of stone flagging and water features – delivers shots of good karma and energising meat-free calories.
☎ 6327 0218 ✉ 445 West Nanjing Rd ⏰ 11am-2pm & 5-10pm Ⓜ Renmin Park/Shimen No1 Rd

Meilongzhen
梅陇镇 (5, C5)
Shanghainese $$
An institutional fixture in the Shanghai restaurant circuit, Meilongzhen has been cooking up a storm since first laying out the chopsticks in the late 1930s.
☎ 6253 5353 ✉ No 22, Lane 1081, West Nanjing Rd ⏰ 11am-2pm & 5-10pm Ⓜ Shimen No 1 Rd

Rendezvous Café
朗迪姆 (5, B6)
American $
Far cheaper and better than TGIF's cardboard patties, the burgers at no-nonsense Rendezvous put the squeeze on over-priced burger bars

---

CHINA IN YOUR HANDS
Flavours from all over the land have drifted into Shanghai, so sample whatever you can without having to travel the vast interior of China. To put some fire in your belly, the **Guyi Hunan Restaurant** (p53) hits the spot. Irresistible **Dongbeiren** (p51) bowls diners over with filling fare from the mighty Manchurian northeast. **Crystal Jade Restaurant** (p53) comes up trumps with its dainty dim sum, and for noodles, **Wuyue Renjia** (opposite) just can't be beat. If Beijing's not in your travel plans, **Quanjude** (p55) brings the best of Peking Duck to town.

THE BEST SHANGHAINESE

With a growing band of branches in town, **Shanghai Uncle** (right) justifiably gets the thumbs up for its local dishes. For atmosphere and history, wreathe yourself in Xujiahui's Jesuit charms with dinner at the **Ye Olde Station Restaurant** (right) but if you need choice Shanghai flavours beyond the witching hour, be birds of a feather with the night owls at **Baoluo Jiulou** (p52). Few find fault with **1221** (p51), which remains a perennial favourite among expat diners.

---

city-wide. Break your overnight fast with the full-on Y28 American Breakfast – or angle later in the day for fish and chips (Y48) or seafood spaghetti (Y48). Other branches around town.
☎ 6247 2307 ✉ 1486 West Nanjing Rd
🕙 7.30am-2.30am
Ⓜ Jing'an Temple

NORTH SHANGHAI

Old Film Café
老电影咖啡馆 (2, C1)
Café $-$$
While doing Duolun Rd Cultural Street (p25), dive in here for a coffee break with all the film buffs and wall-to-wall black-and-white posters from early Chinese cinema.
☎ 5696 4763 ✉ 123 Duolun Rd 🕙 10am-1am
Ⓜ East Baoxing Rd light rail

XUJIAHUI

Coffeelox
诺卡咖啡 (8, B1)
Café $-$$
There's no such thing as a free lunch, but the regularly cut-price dishes – try the scrummy pasta bakes (Y18) or the seafood soup (Y6) –

at this Italian café are the next best thing. One of Shanghai's best value meals, especially if you forgo the coffee beans. Several branches in town.
☎ 6438 7238 ✉ 1988 Huashan Rd 🕙 8.30am-10pm Ⓜ Xujiahui

Shanghai Uncle
海上阿叔 (8, C2)
Shanghainese $$
One of the city's most popular and stylish restaurants for local cuisine, Shanghai Uncle has several branches in town.
☎ 6464 6430 ✉ 211 Tianyueqiao Rd Ⓜ Xujiahui
🕙 11.10am-3.30pm & 5.10-10.30pm

Uighur Restaurant
维吾尔餐厅 (8, A2)
Uighur $-$$
Tacky *Tianshan* water feature aside, the only thing that will tear you away from the fine lamb kebabs, whole shoulder of lamb or spicy *lǎohǔ cài* (spicy tomato, cucumber and onion salad) are the hearty waiters dragging diners off for a quick whirl to accompanying Uighur folk tunes. Several branches in town.
☎ 6468 9188 ✉ 280 Yishan Rd 🕙 10am-2am
Ⓜ Xujiahui/Shanghai Stadium

Xiaofeiyang
小肥羊火锅 (8, B2)
Mongolian Hotpot $-$$
It may take more than a single shot of *báijiǔ* (white spirit) to conjure up the Mongolian grasslands beyond Shanghai's white-tile high rises, but the steaming Mongolian hotpot is the genuine article. Ten branches in town.
☎ 6438 1717 ✉ 169 Nandan Rd 🕙 10am-4am
Ⓜ Xujiahui

Ye Olde Station Restaurant
上海老站 (8, B2)
Shanghainese $$$
This splendid old building, with dark-green shutters and cream exterior, is the former St Ignatius Convent, dating from 1931. Impiously feast on fine Shanghai cuisine, wander down the corridor with its original tiled floor, peruse the old concession-era photos, visit the upstairs chapel and eye up the old train carriages that once conveyed Manchu Empress Cixi and Song Qingling.
☎ 6427 2233 ✉ 80 North Caoxi Rd 🕙 11am-2.30pm & 5.30-10.30pm Ⓜ Xujiahui

Kebabs, Uighur Restaurant

Entertainment

A city of dogged wage-slaves, white-collar aspirants and Bentley-driving nouveau riche, Shanghai craves entertainment as a precious dividend for the punishing office graft and to erase memories of more frugal times. Shanghai's entertainment scene today takes off from where the notorious 'Whore of the Orient' – as the city was once affectionately known – popped lipstick and cigarettes into her handbag for the last time way back in '49.

It may be on a breakneck roll, but don't expect the nightlife to offer particularly good value. With hefty expat salaries in town and a dearth of competitive pricing, drink prices can raise eyebrows. Wine lovers are regularly milked by lawless price tags in bars (and restaurants) and imported beer prices can simply wow if you arrive outside of happy hour. Beer in bars and pubs can cost anything from Y15 per glass/bottle to Y60 plus for imported beers.

Since the early 1990s, Shanghai's cultural scene has been undergoing an urgent makeover and most of your needs will be met, whether it's opera, classical music, rock, jazz, theatre, acrobatics or dance. Acutely sensitive to its perception by the rest of the globe, Shanghai also covets recognition as a city equipped with cutting-edge entertainment facilities and excellent venues have sprung up, including the Shanghai Grand Theatre and the recently completed Oriental Arts Centre. Shanghai has lured several famous acts to town over the past years, including *Cats, The Phantom of the Opera* and *Les Misérables* – all signs of an insatiable appetite for big international productions. Traditional Chinese performance arts – opera and acrobatics – are staples on the tourist circuit and are recommended for first timers to Shanghai and China.

Listings for performances are listed in expat culture magazines, such as *That's Shanghai* and newspapers such as the *Shanghai Daily*. Tickets for cultural performances can be purchased at the **Shanghai Cultural Information & Booking Centre** (SCIBC; ☎ 6217 2426; www.culture.sh.cn; 272 Fengxian Rd). You can also buy tickets for many performances around town from the **Shanghai Centre Theatre** (☎ 6278 8600; 376 West Nanjing Rd).

Elegant performer, Shangai Centre Theatre

BARS, LOUNGES & PUBS

Shanghai's bar scene, simply unheard of 15 years ago, ranges across the full spectrum from rowdy Irish bars to chic lounges. Note: much sidestepping of dross is required to find your bar of choice. New bars – and clubs – fold as rapidly as they appear, only to reopen a few weeks later under new management, in a predictable cycle. Those that stay the course build on the loyalty of regular crowds for the long haul. Expat bars largely constellate along the streets of the French Concession, through Jing'an and in the vicinity of the Bund. Happy hours typically run from 5pm to 8pm.

Bar Rouge (5, J4)
At the prestigious pinnacle of 18 on the Bund, Bar Rouge sees Shanghai's sophisticates convening to sample a fresh, creative drinks menu in one of Shanghai's swishest and choicest bar settings, set to great views.
☎ 6339 1199 ✉ 7th fl, 18 First East Zhongshan Rd ⊙ 8pm-2am Ⓜ Middle Henan Rd

Barbarossa
芭芭露莎会所餐厅 (5, F5)
With its lush and exotic aromas of the Middle East, scattered cushions and hookah pipes, the pondside Barbarossa brings an unexpected dash of Middle Eastern exoticism to Renmin Park.
☎ 6318 0220 ✉ Renmin Park, 231 West Nanjing Rd ⊙ 11am-2am Ⓜ Renmin Park

Big Bamboo (5, B5)
The extrovert sports bar theme gets the heavy-duty makeover in this huge outfit, with a beefy American menu, mammoth sports screen, a dozen plus TV sets, merchandise, a rollicking 2pm to 8pm happy hour, Guinness, pool, darts, DJ and pole position behind the Shanghai Centre.
☎ 6279 4501 🖥 www.big bamboo.cn ✉ 132 Nanyang Rd Ⓜ Jing'an Temple

Blue Frog
蓝蛙 (5, B6)
Far more chic than its South Maoming Rd sibling, this branch of Blue Frog on the new Tongren Rd bar strip is a slick operation, with ambient videos alongside the spirits bottles at the bar, and punters soothed by smooth jazz and chill-out sounds. Lounge music is played on the 3rd floor from 10.30pm and food is served on the 2nd floor.
☎ 6445 6634 ✉ 85 Tongren Rd ⊙ 10am-2am Ⓜ Jing'an Temple

Cloud 9 (6, 3C)
Need a lift at the end of the day? Want to reach an absolute high? Viewing the lights of nocturnal Shanghai from the 87th (and 88th) floor of the Grand Hyatt through the carbonated fizz of a gin and tonic may hoist you to just the right elevation. But the tired, 90s décor could do with a shot of adrenalin.
☎ 5049 1234 ✉ 87th fl, Grand Hyatt, 88 Century Blvd, Pudong ⊙ 6pm-1am Mon-Thu, 6pm-2am Fri, 11am-2am Sat, 11am-1am Sun Ⓜ Lujiazui

Dr Bar
亚科 (3, H2)
If Kraftwerk ever come to Shanghai they will hang out at this dark, pupil-dilating corner of Xintiandi, admiring the clinical, low black furniture and fellow poseurs picked out by candlelight.
☎ 6311 0358 ✉ 15 North Block, Lane 181, Xintiandi, Taicang Rd ⊙ 5pm-2am Ⓜ South Huangpi Rd

The Door
乾门 (7, B2)
It may be way out on a limb in no-frills Hongqiao, but this is one of Shanghai's most elegant and stylish places

Dr Bar in Xintiandi can prescribe just the tonic

for civilised shots of *jiǔjīng* (alcohol) in a choice setting of Chinese porcelain and antiques.

☎ 6295 3737 ✉ 4th fl, 1468 Hongqiao Rd
🕑 6pm-2am

Face (3, G3)
Elegant, soothing, decorated with chinoiserie and manned by polite waiting staff, Face exudes a languorous sophistication and a very non-PC colonial charm. Sundowners on the lawn in summer are a must. Happy hour 5pm to 8pm.

☎ 6466 4328 ✉ Bldg No 4, Ruijin Guest House, 118 Ruijin No 2 Rd 🕑 noon-2am Ⓜ South Shaanxi Rd

Chinese opium bed at Face

Glamour Bar (5, J4)
At the self-conscious epi-centre of Shanghai style, the city's beautiful young things and fashion set appear here

Things pick up a bit later at Glamour Bar at M on the Bund

after hours spent ransacking their wardrobes and fussing obsessively over their hair. Added allure arrives with the live jazz and cabaret.

☎ 6350 9988 ✉ 7th fl, 20 Guangdong Rd, the Bund 🕑 5.30pm-late Ⓜ Middle Henan Rd

The Long Bar
长廊酒吧 (5, B5)
Up the escalators at the Shanghai Centre, the Long Bar remains Shanghai's centre point for the rummy expat bar-fly set, giving the expense account a sound thrashing. When not on stalks gawking at the swim-suit-clad Chinese models (Thursday evening), expat eyes stare into sports TV screens or rapidly emptying wallets.

☎ 6279 8268 ✉ 2nd fl, Shanghai Centre, 1376 West Nanjing Rd 🕑 11am-3am Ⓜ Jing'an Temple

Madam Zung
容夫人 (3, G3)
Overhung with Chinese lanterns, the long, slim, candlelit interior of this French Concession bar offers a master class in elegance, sandwiched between a relax-ing lounge area above and a basement club zone.

☎ 5382 0738 ✉ 4 Xiangshan Rd 🕑 club Thu 9pm-2am, Fri & Sat 9pm-4am, bar 5pm-2am Ⓜ South Shaanxi Rd

Malone's
马龙美式酒楼 (5, B6)
Love it or hate it, this brisk sports bar has been fruitfully ploughing its own furrow for over a decade. Sitting under the glow of sports TV is a cross-section of expat soci-ety, hunched over beers, fish and chips and serenaded by Filipino bands at weekends. The **China Comedy Club** (www.chinacomedyclub.com) brings mirth to comedy-starved expats every month.

☎ 6247 2400 ✉ 255 Tongren Rd 🕑 11am-2am Ⓜ Jing'an Temple

New Heights
新视角 (5, J4)
Rise to the occasion by taking the lift to the rooftop terrace

SOLO IN SHANGHAI

Visiting Shanghai on your Jack Jones won't be a problem and the city naturally caters for solo travellers. If you crave company, **Big Bamboo** (opposite) is as big, loud and extrovert as bars come in town. Almost its exact op-posite, **Dr Bar** (opposite) in Xintiandi has just the right prescription for a more contemplative soiree.

decking of New Heights, a night-time drink (bottle of Hoegaarden Y60), nibbles (bowl of mussels with French fries Y75) and the stellar Pudong lights shimmering seductively over the Huangpu River.
☎ 6321 0909 ⌨ www .threeonthebund.com ✉ 7th fl, Three on the Bund, 3 First East Zhongshan Rd Ⓜ Middle Henan Rd ☽ 10am-2am

O'Malley's
欧玛莉餐厅 (3, D4)
The Irish pub theme straddles China from Qingdao to Chengdu like a giant, synthetic Celtic harp, but few come with such enticing lawns and the classy French Concession perch is grade A.
☎ 6437 0667 ⌨ www .omalleysirishpub.com ✉ 42 Taojiang Rd ☽ 11am-2am Ⓜ Changshu Rd ♿

Time Passage
昨天今天明天 (3, B3)
If you like cheap beer and an undemanding, lived-in ambience, this student-set bar has been charting its chronological passage since 1994. Despite the address, the

bar is actually on Caojiayan Rd (next door to the tennis court). Live music – often impromptu – takes to the air every Friday and Saturday after 10.30pm. Bargain beer every Tuesday night.
☎ 6240 2588 ✉ 83 Huashan Rd ☽ 5.30pm-2am Mon-Thu, 5pm-2am Fri-Sun Ⓜ Jiangsu Rd

CLASSICAL MUSIC

With several excellent high-profile venues, Shanghai hosts regular performances from the Shanghai Symphony Orchestra, the Shanghai Broadcast Symphony Orchestra and the Shanghai Philharmonic Orchestra. See Bandu Cabin (p57) for details of their traditional Chinese music concerts.

Jinjiang Hotel
锦江饭店 (3, F2)
Classical music concerts are held on the first Sunday of every month in the Grand Hall.
☎ 6258 2582 ✉ 59 South Maoming Rd $ Y50 Ⓜ South Shaanxi Rd

Oriental Art Centre
上海东方艺术中心
Designed by Paul Andreu and opened to much fanfare in 2004, Pudong's spectacular culture complex embraces a 2000-seat concert hall, an experimental theatre and a cinema.
☎ 6854 7757 ✉ 425 Dingxiang Rd Ⓜ Shanghai Science and Technology Museum

Shanghai Concert Hall
上海音乐厅 (5, G5)
Equipped with fine acoustics and recently relocated 66m southeast of its former location, this 75-year-old building is the venue for regular performances by orchestras including the Shanghai Symphony Orchestra and the Shanghai Broadcasting Symphony Orchestra.
☎ 6386 9153 ⌨ www .shanghaiconcerthall.org ✉ 523 East Yan'an Rd $ Y20-200 Ⓜ Renmin Square

Shanghai Conservatory of Music
上海音乐学院 (3, E3)
Musical performances (from classical to traditional

SHANGHAI PIRATES
Despite blasts of official hot air to the contrary, the pirate DVD market in Shanghai – and nationwide – is rampant. Pirate DVD outlets take over entire alleys, with hawkers setting up trestle tables willy-nilly as policemen stroll by stifling yawns. Retailing for Y7, pirate DVD quality is often shoddy (around one in three discs is unwatchable), but they can be swapped and the industry constantly ups its standards to meet a ravenous demand. Limp-wristed crackdowns precede sensitive events (eg the Shanghai International Film Festival), but the political will to enforce a ban just isn't there.

Opera, musicals, ballet. Shanghai Grand Theatre has it all

Chinese music) are held here at 7.15pm (typically on Saturdays and Sundays, but other days as well). Tickets are available from the ticket office just north of the conservatory, amid the musical instrument shops, at 8 Fenyang Rd.
☎ 6431 1792 ✉ 20 Fenyang Rd $ Y80-380 Ⓜ Changshu Rd/South Shaanxi Rd

Shanghai Grand Theatre
上海大剧院 (5, F5)
The distinctively styled landmark theatre is equipped with three theatres, and stages musicals, ballet, operas, music concerts and drama productions.
☎ 6372 8701 🖳 www .shgtheatre.com ✉ 300 Renmin Ave $ Y80-280 plus Ⓜ Renmin Square

CINEMAS

Shanghai's cinema industry is sabotaged by both rampant DVD piracy and uncompetitive pricing, which keep bums off seats. Long delays in screenings for the 20-odd Western films projected onto the big screen further faze audiences. With the latest Hollywood releases steaming off the pirate press and on DVD hawkers' stalls months before their official China release, it's a miracle anyone still goes to the movies. Cinemas miraculously not only refuse to go belly up, however, but new theatres open yearly. The 10-day **Shanghai International Film Festival** (www .siff.com) comes to town in June to restore precious lifeblood to a sickly industry. The cinemas listed here all screen English language films. Tickets tend to hover in the Y40 to Y60 price range, but morning, late evening and Tuesday (whole-day) screenings are often cheaper. When buying a ticket, check whether the film is in the original language.

Cathay Theatre
国泰电影院 (3, F2)
This gorgeous old, brick Art Deco fixture on Huaihai Rd screens occasional English language films.
☎ 5404 2095 ✉ 870 Central Huaihai Rd $ Y40-50 Ⓜ South Shaanxi Rd

Kodak Cinema World
超级电影世界 (8, B2)
This four screen cinema in bustling Xujiahui has a film club that meets once a month for screenings of independent cinema.
☎ 6426 8181 🖳 www .cinemaworld.kodak.com ✉ Metro City, 1111 Zhaojiabang Rd, Xujiahui
$ Y40-60 Ⓜ Xujiahui

Paradise Cinema City
永华电影城 (8, B1)
Large nine-screen cinema in Xujiahui with regular Hollywood offerings, the latest Hong Kong and Chinese movies and a large variety of screening times.
☎ 6407 6622 ext 8002 ✉ 6th fl, Grand Gateway, 1 Hongqiao Rd, Xujiahui
$ Y50-60 Ⓜ Xujiahui

Shanghai Film Art Centre
上海影城 (3, A5)
This cinema on the corner of picturesque, leafy Xinhua Rd serves as the main venue for the Shanghai International Film Festival.
☎ 6280 4088 ✉ 160 Xinhua Rd $ Y50-60 Ⓜ Zhongshan Park

Peace Cinema
和平影都 (5, F4)
Excellently located cinema equipped with an IMAX screen on the eastern side of Renmin Square.
☎ 6361 2898 ✉ 290 Central Xizang Rd $ Y50-60 Ⓜ Renmin Park/Renmin Square

Shanghai Stellar Megamedia Cinema City
星美正大影城 (6, B3)
Seven-screen cinema on the virtually deserted top floor

of the Thai-owned Pudong monster mall.
☎ 5047 2025 ✉ 8th fl, Super Brand Mall, 168 Lujiazui Rd $ Y50-60 Ⓜ Lujiazui

Studio City
环艺电影城 (5, C5)
Tenth-floor, six-screen multi-plex located in Westgate Mall.
☎ 6218 2173 ✉ 10th fl, Westgate Mall, 1038 West Nanjing Rd $ Y50-60 Ⓜ Shimen No 1 Rd

UME International Cineplex
新天地国际影城 (3, H2)
Huge cinema rising up at the south end of the Xintiandi *shíkùmén* restaurant, bar and retail hub.
☎ 6384 1122 ext 807 🖥 www.ume.com.cn ✉ 4th fl, No 6, Lane 123, Xingye Rd $ Y50-60 Ⓜ South Huangpi Rd

ROCK, JAZZ & BLUES

Judged by international norms, Shanghai's live music scene is pitiful and no reason to bring one into town. Few

Rockin' out at Ark

'Got the expat blues', Cotton Club, French Concession

international bands pass through Shanghai, and those that do tend to drift over from the innocuous middle of the road (Elton John etc). Filipino bands aside, the live music bar is slowly being raised, however, as the city upgrades its interest in live tunes.

Ark
亚科 (3, H2)
With enough room to swing an elephant, Ark offers mas-sive head room, a smart layout and nightly rock and metal, all in a smart Xintiandi locale.
☎ 6326 8008 🖥 www.ark-lh.com ✉ 5 North Block, Lane 181, Xintiandi, Taicang Rd ⏰ 5.30pm-late Ⓜ South Huangpi Rd

House of Blues and Jazz
(3, F3)
From the live jazz numbers, in-house band, to the walls plastered with jazz legends, this place is wall-to-wall bop.
☎ 6437 5280 ✉ 158 South Maoming Rd ⏰ 4pm-2am Tue-Sun Ⓜ South Shaanxi Rd

Cotton Club (3, D4)
Decked out in wood and brass with black and white

stills of jazz greats fixed to the walls, the old-timer Cotton Club snaps its fingers nightly to soothing doses of live jazz and blues.
☎ 6437 7110 ✉ 1428 Huaihai Rd ⏰ 7pm-3am; live music 9pm-12am Sun-Thu, 9.30pm-1.30am Fri & Sat Ⓜ Changshu Rd

JZ Club
爵士俱乐部 (3, C4)
The cheesy décor and Y50 draught beer (no happy hour) is a sure-fire turn-off so only come here for the live jazz sounds, which packs in the faithful from 10pm.
☎ 6431 0269 ✉ 46 West Fuxing Rd ⏰ live music from 10pm Ⓜ Changshu Rd/Hengshan Rd

Tang Hui
堂会 (3, A5)
Overlooked by posters of Kurt Cobain and Bob Marley, this dark, candlelit French Con-cession borderlands bar isn't about sophistication (wobbly tables, concrete floor) but the music – jam sessions, punk, rock – puts the Filipino band schlock on pause.
☎ 6238 6162 ✉ 13 Xingfu Rd ⏰ 8pm-2am Ⓜ Zhong-shan Park/Xujiahui

CLUBS

Babyface (3, F4)
South Maoming Rd lounge club that slots in nicely with Shanghai's image-conscious, uber-chic crowd fretfully keeping tabs on who's wearing what.
☎ 6445 2330 ⊠ 180 South Maoming Rd ☽ 8.30pm-3am Ⓜ South Shaanxi Rd

California Club (3, G2)
Winning the hearts, minds, hips and legs of stylish Chinese locals and the work/play hard expat Shanghai set, this Fuxing Park club is spot on with its list of international DJs and funky, image-conscious clientele.
☎ 5383 2328 ⊠ 2 Gaolan Rd ☽ 9pm-2am Sun-Thu & 9pm-4am Fri & Sat Ⓜ South Huangpi Rd/South Shaanxi

La Fabrique (3, G4)
For the modern and sophisticated set, La Fabrique fuses dining, clubbing (house, up beat dance) and sleek design to bring a sharp, innovative edge to Shanghai's rapidly evolving and time-sensitive club scene.
☎ 6415 1600 ⊠ Bldg 7, 8-10 Central Jianguo Rd ☽ 10.30pm-4am Wed-Sat Ⓜ South Shaanxi Rd/South Huangpi Rd

Mint (5, B5)
Gently rattling the windows of the 2nd floor of Hudec's Green House – a pile of 1930s Bauhaus nostalgia in need of a lick of paint – Mint is a languid club for lounging to smooth chill-out sounds, Latin house and funk (happy hour 7pm to 9pm).
☎ 6247 9666 ⊠ 2nd fl, 333 Tongren Rd Ⓢ Y100

☽ 6pm-2am Mon-Thu, 9pm-7am Fri & Sat Ⓜ Jing'an Temple

Paramount Ballroom
百乐门 (5, A6)
Completed in 1932 at a cost of 700, 000 tael of silver, the Paramount was Shanghai's first casino, before emerging as a den of iniquity during the Japanese occupation (and later serving as the Hongdu Cinema). The interior of the Art Deco building has been revamped and nostalgic 1930s Shanghai dancing shows are held nightly at 6.30pm, with ballroom dancing a further nightly fixture.
☎ 6249 8866 ⊠ 218 Yuyuan Rd Ⓢ Y100 Ⓜ Jing'an Temple

Pegasus (3, J1)
Somehow managing to be both swish and full-on in its convergence of huge scale and smooth design, Pegasus is still one of Shanghai's most popular clubs, with massive Thursday hip hop nights. Revellers lounge at window-side seats while a well-equipped smoking room is at hand for cigars and recuperative shots of liquor.
☎ 5385 8187 ⊠ 2nd fl, Golden Bell Plaza, 98 Central Huaihai Rd ☽ 6pm-4am Ⓜ South Huangpi Rd

Pu-J's (6, B3)
The Grand Hyatt's extravagant entertainment multiplex brings you venues to suit your mood: jazz, live music, dance and karaoke.
☎ 5049 1234 ext 8732 ⊠ Podium 3, Jinmao Tower, 88 Century Blvd ☽ 7pm-2am Fri & Sat, 7pm-1am Sun-Thu Ⓢ Y100 Ⓜ Lujiazui

AND THE BUND PLAYED ON
Chalking up an average age of 76 – *older* than the Stones – the six-man **Peace Hotel Jazz Band** (Map 5, J3; ☎ 6321 6888; Peace Hotel Bar, Peace Hotel, 20 East Nanjing Rd; Y50; ☽ 8pm) first started cranking out their jazz classics in 1980. Two of the old-timers – including the band's founder and trumpet player Zhou Wanrong – are former members of China's first all-Chinese band fronted by Jimmy King in the 1940s, which had a regular slot at the Paramount (right). The veterans' repertoire is a nostalgic, if undemanding, catalogue of 1930s and 1940s numbers.

Rojam (3, H1)
This place may be immense, but it still packs in weekend clubbers at density levels only otherwise achieved by carriages on the No 2 line

metro during the 9am crush hour.
☎ 6390 7181 ✉ 4th fl, Hong Kong Plaza, 283 Central Huaihai Rd ⏲ 8.30pm-2am Ⓜ South Huangpi Rd

SPECIAL EVENTS
January & February
Spring Festival: commencing on the first day of the first moon of the lunar calendar, the Chinese New Year is marked by fireworks and a week-long celebration. To be held 29 January 2006; 18 February 2007; 7 February 2008.

March & April
Birthday of Guanyin: on the 19th day of the second lunar month, the birthday of the Goddess of Compassion is celebrated in Buddhist temples city-wide.
Qingming Festival: Shanghai really goes to town on the Tomb-Sweeping Festival, when tombs of deceased relatives are tended. Held on 5 April (4 April in leap years) every year.

May & June
Dragon Boat Festival: commemorating the death of 3rd-century BC poet-statesman Qu Yuan, dragon boat races have recently included expat teams. To be held 31 May 2006; 19 June 2007; 8 June 2008.
Shanghai International Music Festival: an assorted gaggle of bands and sounds descends on Shanghai in May.

June
Shanghai International Film Festival (SIFF): mixed bag of Chinese film and foreign films from Korea to Hollywood.

July
Shanghai Beer Festival: the Bund is awash with the summer aromas of hops and yeast in late July.

September & October
Mid-Autumn Festival: a traditional time for families to get together and eat moon cakes. To be held 6 October 2006; 25 September 2007; 14 September 2008
Formula One: high-octane fumes and smoking rubber come to town September/October.

November
Shanghai International Arts Festival: major month-long cultural highpoint of the year; bringing music, theatre and artistic performances to Shanghai's top venues.

THEATRE & ACROBATICS

If you want to know what's walking the boards in Shanghai, consult the expat English language magazines for details.

Lyceum Theatre
兰心大剧院 (3, F2)
The recently renovated brick Lyceum dates back to 1867, but the theatre moved to the current building – one of Shanghai's oldest and most architecturally interesting theatres – in 1931. The theatre stages a variety of performances, including acrobatics, magic shows, ballet, Chinese opera and Shaolin *gönfu*. It's worth popping in to have a look at the renovated lobby interior, where there is a small café.
☎ 6256 4832 ✉ 57 South Maoming Rd Ⓜ South Shaanxi Rd

Shanghai Centre Theatre
上海商城剧院 (5, B5)
The city's most popular joint-popping acrobatic display takes place here nightly, performed by the famous Shanghai Acrobatics Theatre. Acts include plate-spinning and *göngfu*.
☎ 6279 8663 ✉ 1376 West Nanjing Rd 💲 Y50-100 ⏲ 7.30pm Ⓜ Jing'an Temple

Shanghai Circus World
上海马戏团
Located in the north of town, this impressive modern complex has regular body-bending performances from the Shanghai Acrobatic

Troupe, animal shows and spectacular performances. Phone or check the website for details.

☎ 5665 6622 ext 2091
🖥 www.circus-world.com
✉ 2266 Gonghexin Rd
$ Y50-280 ⏲ 7.30pm

Shanghai Dramatic Arts Centre

上海话剧中心 (3, B3)
This theatre stages a range of local and international drama (performances in both English and Chinese) and occasional productions of Chinese opera.

☎ 6473 4567 or 6433 5133
✉ 288 Anfu Rd ⏲ 7.30pm
$ Y80-800 Ⓜ Changshu Rd

Yunfeng Theatre

云峰剧场 (5, A6)
Set back from West Beijing Rd in a courtyard just west of a delightful row of old cottages, this ugly-duckling theatre offers nightly doses of acrobatics, with occasional Chinese musicals and drama.

☎ 6258 2258 ✉ 1700 West Beijing Rd $ Tickets from Y150 ⏲ 7.30pm
Ⓜ Jing'an Temple

Shanghai Centre Theatre

GAY & LESBIAN SHANGHAI

With its calling to promote spiritual civilisation, the People's Republic takes a dim view of homosexuality. In response, gay and lesbian appetites in Shanghai are largely subterranean and homosexual behaviour in public is clandestine and low-key. Although still undeveloped, a growing bar and club scene provides an energetic sanctuary for gays citywide.

Dream Star

French Concession gay and lesbian bar with dancing and frolicking in the onsite swimming pool.

☎ 6471 2887 ✉ Basement, 307 South Shaanxi Rd
⏲ 7.30pm-late Ⓜ South Shaanxi Rd

Home & Bar (3, G3)

Newly arrived gays from other parts of China and abroad tend to make this their first port of call, Shanghai's premier and best-known gay bar near Fuxing Park (admission charge at weekends).

☎ 5382 0373 ✉ 18 Gaolan Rd ⏲ 8pm to late Ⓜ South Shaanxi Rd

Eddy's Bar (3, B5)

Easing into its second decade, Eddy's Bar attracts a slightly more mature Chinese and international gay crowd with inexpensive drinks and neat décor.

☎ 6282 0521 🖥 www .eddys-bar.com ✉ 1877 Central Huaihai Rd ⏲ 8pm-2am Ⓜ Hengshan Rd

Vogue (3, C3)

Despite its profile as one of Shanghai's leading gay venues, Vogue is buried down an alley near the junction of Changle Rd and Wulumuqi Rd. Mixed crowd and packed at weekends.

☎ 6248 8985 ✉ 946 Changle Rd ⏲ 8pm-2am
Ⓜ Changshu Rd

CHINESE OPERA

Yifu Theatre

逸夫舞台 (5, G5)
The theatre stages a variety of regional operatic styles, including Beijing opera (jīngjù), Kunju opera (kūnqǔ) and Yue opera (yuèjù). A shop in the foyer sells CD recordings of these operatic works.

☎ 6351 4668 ✉ 701 Fuzhou Rd $ Tickets Y20-280 ⏲ 7.15pm Ⓜ Renmin Square

Kunju Opera House

上海昆剧团 (3, F4)
Dating back over 600 years, lyrical and dance-oriented Kunju (kūnqǔ) opera emerged from Kunshan in Jiangsu province. Performances are held here on Saturdays.

☎ 6437 1012 ✉ 9 Shaoxing Rd $ Tickets Y20-50
⏲ 1.30pm Sat Ⓜ South Shaanxi Rd

Majestic Theatre

美琪大剧院 (5, C5)
This is Shanghai's oldest theatre, with musical and ballet productions and performances of Chinese opera.

☎ 6217 2426 or 6217 4409 ✉ 66 Jiangning Rd
⏲ matinee performances; evening 7.15pm $ Y60-800+ Ⓜ Shimen No 1 Rd

SPORT

An energetic expat community fields competitions in virtually the full gamut of sports from Gaelic football, through to darts, fencing, ice hockey, rugby, squash, volleyball and beyond. For complete listings and contact details, check the English language expat magazines.

Football

China is pathologically obsessed with the beautiful game. Sadly, the dearth of green space in Shanghai – and other Chinese cities – is a sliding tackle on efforts to cultivate local talent. The football pitches that exist are expensive, further alienating talented youngsters. The Chinese league is moreover

Nerves of steel, Shanghai Stadium

mired by controversies over match fixings and other corrupt goings-on, although Shanghai Shenhua is one of China's leading teams. The **Shanghai Stadium** (Map 8, B4; ☎ 6438 5200; 1111 North Caoxi Rd; tickets from Y50) and **Hongkou Stadium** (☎ 6540 0009; 715 Dongtiyuhui Rd; tickets from Y50) are the principal venues, with regular match fixtures. The **Shanghai International Football League** (www.eteams.com/sifl) is an expat league of teams that plays every Saturday during the season at Tianma Country Club, around an hour's drive west of town. Attendance is free and those keen to play can sign up (shin pads mandatory).

Motor racing

The slick new **Shanghai International Circuit** (☎ 6956 6999; www.icsh .sh.cn; 2000 Yining Rd, Jiading) hosts several high profile motor racing competitions, including the hotly contested **Formula One Grand Prix** (Y160 to Y3980) in September, China Circuit Championship and **Moto Grand Prix** (Y30 to Y1880).

Other Sports

The gruelling Shanghai International Marathon heaves in lungfuls of ozone come November. The 42km course starts at the Bund and concludes at Shanghai Stadium. For tennis fans, the annual Shanghai Open is the largest competition. Dragon boat races are held on Dianshan Lake in training for competitions during the Dragon Boat Festival (p66).

Shooting some hoops, Shanghai Stadium

Sleeping

Enjoying an 80% occupancy rate in 2004, when close on four million visitors breezed into town, Shanghai's five-star hotels are cashing in on a business and tourist travel boom. With 2003 – the year of SARS – largely forgotten, Shanghai is instead gearing up for Expo 2010's estimated influx of 70 million visitors. The hotel industry in Shanghai is in fine fettle, so it is advisable to book ahead.

You will be spoilt for choice, albeit only at the top end of the market. International chain hotels make up the cream of Shanghai's five-star hotels: slick, modern and opulent, but possessing little history or stature. Shanghai's historic hotels – such as the Peace Hotel and the Park Hotel – have more charm, yet few achieve international five-star standards and service is sometimes sullen, so treat some five-star rankings with suspicion. Lower on the rack-rate ladder, the midrange market boasts several hotels with personality and a story to tell. Promotions and discounts mean that you can usually get a room well below the rack rate.

ROOM RATES

The categories indicate the cost per night of a standard double room in high season (May to September; other peak times: first week of May, first week of October and Chinese New Year).

Deluxe	Y2000-2400 (US$250-300)
Top End	Y1200-2000 (US$150-250)
Midrange	Y650-1200 (US$80-150)
Budget	Y50-650 (US$6-80)

Deluxe, top-end and many midrange hotels add a 15% service charge to quoted rates. Hotels almost never charge the rack rate and discounts of up to 50% are possible, but more often around 20%–40% are typical.

Inviting, roomy doubles at St Regis

At five-star hotels you should expect excellent sport, recreational and shopping facilities, a swimming pool, a wide selection of fine restaurants, ATMs, and exquisitely furnished rooms equipped with the usual five-star amenities. Superior comfort should also be available on executive floors, which typically provide free drinks upon arrival and in the afternoon, complimentary breakfast and business facilities. Most four- and five-star hotels offer in-room broadband Internet, although this is rarely free of charge. Future additions to the deluxe circuit include the Regent Shanghai, due to open in late 2005.

The provision of decent midrange hotels in Shanghai is inadequate and most – apart from the few historic hotels which cater to international guests – are bland, unexciting and have problems conversing in English. Hotels at this level may have a Western restaurant and possibly a swimming pool and bar. Rooms will come with air-con, satellite or cable TV, telephone, kettle, mini-bar and broadband connection (typically not free).

The budget market remains underrepresented, with foreigners still shamefully barred from many of the cheap guesthouses (although speakers of Chinese are admitted more readily). As a result, Shanghai stays can take gaping chunks from tight budgets. Backpackers have only a few places to go, but what is available is clean and comfortable, and the list is growing.

DELUXE

Four Seasons Hotel Shanghai
四季大酒店 (5, D5)
A relative newcomer to the Shanghai luxury market, the sumptuousness of the Four Seasons lobby extends throughout the hotel to embrace such extravagant details as the 24-hour butler service.
☎ 6256 8888 🖵 www .fourseasons.com ✉ 500 Weihai Rd Ⓜ Shimen No 1 Rd ⟨ good ✕ ♨

Grand Hyatt
上海金茂君悦大酒店 (6, C3)
The highest hotel in the world above ground level, the astronomical Grand Hyatt similarly tops the highly competitive Shanghai hotel league. The views are flabbergasting, the rooms are gorgeous (keeping the glass sinks clean must be a chore for chambermaids), the atrium is simply mind-blowing and dining and entertaining options are

If this makes you dizzy, wait till you climb it, Grand Hyatt

impressively opulent. It's continuously booked out, so reserve well ahead.
☎ 5049 1234 🖵 www .hyatt.com ✉ 88 Century Blvd Ⓜ Lujiazui ⟨ OK ✕ ♨

JC Mandarin Shanghai
上海锦沧文化大酒店 (5, C6)
Built on the ruins of the Burlington Hotel, the Meritus-managed JC Mandarin offers elegantly furnished rooms with a full range of in-room facilities and a stylish choice of dining options.
☎ 6279 1888 🖵 www .jcmandarin.com ✉ 1225 West Nanjing Rd Ⓜ Shimen No 1 Rd ⟨ OK ♨

JW Marriott
万豪酒店 (5, E5)
The flagship Marriott extends over 23 floors in Puxi's most thrilling and eye-catching edifice – Tomorrow Square – soaring above Renmin Square. The fully equipped and spacious rooms come with laptop safes and stunning views, while the bathtub's hydraulic massage is a stress-busting bonus. Taking a leaf from the Grand Hyatt book, the hotel boasts the world's highest library.
☎ 5359 4969 🖵 www .marriott.com ✉ 37th fl to 60th fl, Tomorrow Square, 399 West Nanjing Rd Ⓜ Renmin Square ⟨ OK ✕ restaurant/café

Portman Ritz-Carlton
上海波特曼丽嘉大酒店 (5, B5)
A gilt-edged quality benchmark in Shanghai's congested five-star hotel market, given extra gloss

in 1999 with a spangling US$30 million refit price tag, the luxurious Portman Ritz-Carlton is the fabulous centrepiece of the Shanghai Centre.
☎ 6279 8888 🖵 www .ritzcarlton.com ✉ 1376 West Nanjing Rd Ⓜ Jing'an Temple ✕ restaurant/bar ♨

St Regis
上海瑞吉红塔大酒店
The gracefully designed and clutter-free lobby is a taster for the flawless doubles, Shanghai's roomiest at 48 sq metres. Spacious bathrooms are accessed via swish sliding doors, the taps are lined along the side of the bath, the shower has a Rainforest shower head and broadband comes free. And don't forget the butler service and ladies only floor, while noting the funky lift buttons mounted on glass pillars. In all aspects bar location and views, this is Shanghai's best hotel.
☎ 5050 4567 🖵 www .stregis.com/shanghai ✉ 889 Dongfang Rd Ⓜ Dongfang Rd ⟨ OK ✕ Danieli's (p56) ♨

Westin Shanghai
威斯汀大饭店 (5, H4)
A short hop from the Bund, the Westin's stylish and spacious rooms come with the Westin Heavenly Bed, Rainforest showers and telephones in bathrooms. The Banyan tree spa is perfect for decompressing after a long flight.
☎ 6335 1888 ✉ Bund Centre, 88 Central Henan Rd 🖵 www.westin.com Ⓜ Middle Henan Rd ⟨ ✕ ♨

88 Xintiandi

88新天地 (3, H2)

Luxurious comfort with gorgeous traditional Chinese-styling awaits at every turn in this Xintiandi hotel at the heart of Shanghai's French Concession. The well-appointed rooms – some offering lake views – include free broadband and full kitchen facilities, but the hotel is already showing slight signs of wear and tear.

☎ 5383 8833 🖳 www .88xintiandi.com ✉ 380 South Huangpi Rd Ⓜ South Huangpi Rd Ⓧ

TOP END

Bund Hotel

金外滩宾馆 (5, G5)

The name's a gross misnomer considering it's a good 15-minute walk to the Bund, but this glittering new hotel – complete with a sparkling gold and marble foyer – has lovely rooms, smiling keen-to-impress service and a fine location just east of Renmin Square.

☎ 6352 2000 ✉ 525 Guangdong Rd Ⓜ Renmin Square Ⓧ restaurant

Courtyard by Marriott

上海齐鲁万怡大酒店

The wanting exterior of the four-star Courtyard conceals a stylish and comfortable interior, with a birdcage at the heart of the lobby, behind which a space-dividing lattice screen also finds service as a bar. All rooms were due for new beds in 2005, with 100 extra rooms to be added.

☎ 6886 7886 🖳 www .marriott.com ✉ 838

Dongfang Rd Ⓜ Dongfang Rd Ⓧ restaurant/café

Hengshan Moller Villa

衡山马勒别墅饭店 (3, E1)

The crazy brickwork, Never-Never Land turrets, gorgeous lawn and impeccable interior features sees the few rooms in the main building of the standout Hengshan Moller Villa constantly booked out, so book weeks ahead or you will have to settle for the modern block located behind.

☎ 6247 8881 🖳 www .mollervilla.com ✉ 30 South Shaanxi Rd Ⓜ Shimen No 1 Rd/Jing'an Temple/South Shaanxi Rd Ⓧ restaurant/café

Hilton Shanghai

静安希尔顿大酒店 (3, C2)

Long in the tooth it may be and the brown granite lobby effect is weary in parts, but the towering Hilton Shanghai remains remarkably popular

Hengshan Moller Villa

with business travellers. The Jing'an location has kept it well in the running, while upgrades and excellent service further hoists it up the rankings. People on the Water (p55), located in the basement, is a new and stylish Ningbo seafood restaurant.

☎ 6248 0000 🖳 www .hilton.com ✉ 250 Huashan Rd Ⓜ Jing'an Temple Ⓧ People on the Water ♿ good ⓧ

SERVICED APARTMENTS

If staying long-term in Shanghai, consider staying in one of Shanghai's many serviced apartments, where facilities should range from supermarkets, crèches, dry-cleaners, swimming pool, tennis courts and sometimes on-site medical clinics. The **Shanghai Centre Serviced Apartments** (Map 5, B5; ☎ 6279 8502; www.shang haicentre.com; 1376 West Nanjing Rd) brings you the extensive facilities of the Shanghai Centre, with apartments ranging from studios (daily/weekly $125/875) to three-bedroom flats (daily/weekly $275/1925); minimum stay five nights. If you need to live in Pudong, the fully equipped **Ascott Pudong** (Map 6, C2; ☎ 6886 0088; 3 Central Pudong Ave) provides luxury long-term accommodation from one-bedroom (daily/monthly $167/3663) to three-bedroom (daily/monthly $267/5550) apartments.

Holiday Inn Pudong
浦东假日酒店
Next to the St Regis, the Holiday Inn is popular with business travellers and regular discounts make room prices very competitive. The lobby and décor is unremarkable, with a trio of classical musicians giving some lift, while Flanagan's pub on the ground floor beckons with hearty pints and sports TV. ☎ 5830 6666; toll free 800 830 1123 💻 www.holiday-inn.com ✉ 899 Dongfang Rd Ⓜ Dongfang Rd ✖ restaurant/café ♿ OK

Hotel Equatorial
国际贵都大酒店 (3, C2)
Manned by professional staff, this has been transformed over recent years into a well-managed four-star hotel. Rooms are to a good standard and were being refurbished at the time of writing. Has wireless high-speed Internet access in lobby. ☎ 6248 1688 💻 www.equatorial.com/sha ✉ 65 West Yan'an Rd Ⓜ Jing'an Temple ✖ restaurant/café

Jinjiang Hotel
锦江饭店 (3, F2)
One of Shanghai's most historic hotels, the old-world, slightly scuffed, but elegant five-star Jinjiang straggles somewhat behind the slicker competition. Nonetheless, staying here – either in the Cathay Building, the recently refurbished and cheaper Jin Nan building or the magnificent Grosvenor House, puts you in the heart of the French Concession. ☎ 6258 2582 ✉ 59 South Maoming Rd Ⓜ South Shaanxi Rd ✖ restaurant/bar

Okura Garden Hotel
花园饭店 (3, F2)
The Okura Garden Hotel deserves special attention for its location on the site of the old French Club, the Art Deco styling of its lobbies and grand ballroom, and the very polite staff. Rooms are looking slightly weary, but current renovations should restore freshness and vitality. Most guests here hail from Japan. ☎ 6415 1111 💻 www.gardenhotelshanghai.com ✉ 58 South Maoming Rd Ⓜ South Shaanxi Rd ✖

Park Hotel
国际饭店 (5, F4)
One of Shanghai's finest Art Deco monuments and Shanghai's tallest building until the 1980s, the Park Hotel dates back to 1934 (when Renmin Park still thundered to the sound of racehorses). The rooms here are comfortable enough and the bathrooms clean. Try to book a room with a view overlooking Nanjing Rd. ☎ 6327 5225 💻 www.parkhotel.com.cn ✉ 170 West Nanjing Rd Ⓜ Renmin Park ✖ restaurant/bar

Interior of Park Hotel

Stairway of the Peace Hotel

Peace Hotel
和平饭店 (5, J3)
The Peace Hotel – the city's premier historic lodging – is a battered warhorse alongside Shanghai's increasingly purebred rivals. The hotel has quality control issues of an institutional nature that leave a whopping dent in its crown, but its historical features and location allows it to exploit a much-coveted market niche. ☎ 6321 6888 ✉ 20 East Nanjing Rd 💻 www.shanghaipeacehotel.com Ⓜ Middle Henan Rd ✖ restaurant/bar (Peace Hotel Old Jazz Bar; see p65)

Pudong Shangri-La
浦东香格里拉大酒店 (6, B3)
Its 28 floors may give it Lilliputian stature in this land of architectural giants, but that's before you spot the spangling new V-topped tower behind, bringing this fabulous hotel's complement of rooms to almost 1000. The Shangri-La formula produces a restrained elegance without the gaudiness of some top-league hotels and doubles are elegantly modern, with

AIRPORT HOTELS

For travellers arriving at Hongqiao Airport, the **Marriott Hotel Hongqiao** (Map 2, A3; ☎ 6237 6000; www.marriott.com; 2270 Hongqiao Rd), 6km from the airport, has a full range of five-star facilities. For the more budget-conscious, **Motel 168** (☎ 6401 9188; 1148 Wuzhong Rd; p75) is a mere 3km from Hongqiao Airport. In Pudong, the **Ramada Pudong Airport** (☎ 3849 4949; www.ramadaairportpd.com; 1100 Qihang Rd) has a decent range of luxury amenities. Luxury hotels regularly provide shuttle buses to and from both airports.

shower and bath. Bund views are worth the small extra outlay.
☎ 6882 8888 ▢ www.shangri-la.com ✉ 33 Fucheng Rd Ⓜ Lujiazui ✗ restaurant/bar

Seagull Hotel

海鸥饭店 (5, J2)
Popular with Japanese and Russian businessmen, the Seagull – its lobby a gaudy blitz of gold and marble – is small enough to seem intimate and enjoys an excellent perch north of Suzhou Creek, with enviable views over the river to Pudong. Standard rooms may not be large, but are being renovated from top to bottom, with completion slated for late 2005.
☎ 6325 1500 ▢ www.seagull-hotel.com ✉ 60 Huangpu Rd Ⓜ Middle Henan Rd

Ruijin Guesthouse

瑞金宾馆 (3, G3)
The former Morris Estate, this historic guesthouse consists of converted former villas. The garden setting is delightful and what the French Concession is all about. The occasionally slipshod service

is a kink in an otherwise smooth operation.
☎ 6472 5222 ▢ www.shedi.net.cn/outedi/ruijin ✉ 118 Ruijin No 2 Rd Ⓜ South Shaanxi Rd ✗ Xiao Nan Guo, Lan Na Thai and Face bar

Taiyuan Villa

太原别墅 (3, E5)
Built in 1920, this villa hotel once served as Jiang Qing's – Mao's other half – Shanghai residence, before she was packed off to prison and eventual suicide. The gorgeous setting is peacefully nostalgic, although facilities are limited.
☎ 6471 6688 ✉ 160 Taiyuan Rd Ⓜ Hengshan Rd ✗ restaurant

MIDRANGE

Broadway Mansions

上海大厦 (5, J2)
Topped with a Bayer sign and looming over Suzhou Creek north of the Bund, the 1930s Art Deco Broadway Mansions enjoys a splendid location. Rooms come in varying degrees of refurbishment, but the views out front require little improvement.
☎ 6324 6260 ▢ www.broadwaymansions.com ✉ 20 North Suzhou Rd Ⓜ Middle Henan Rd ✗ restaurant/bar

City Hotel

城市酒店 (3, E2)
The chief appeal of this recently renovated four-star business hotel is the reasonable room rates and the central location.
☎ 6255 1133 ✉ 5-7 South Shaanxi Rd ▢ www.cityhotelshanghai.com Ⓜ South Shaanxi Rd ✗ restaurant

Hengshan Hotel

衡山宾馆 (3, C6)
Formerly the Picardie Apartments, recent refurbishment has restored some of the original class to this well-located French Concession

The very European Ruijin Guest House, French Concession

hotel, with the 'A' superior rooms being particularly spacious.

☎ 6437 7050 🖳 www .hotelhengshan.com ✉ 534 Hengshan Rd Ⓜ Hengshan Rd 🍽 restaurant

Jinchen Hotel

金晨大酒店 (3, F2)

The recently restored rooms in the excellently located, seven-storey brick Jinchen are clean and tastefully furnished (with free broadband), spic and span bathrooms (with deep baths). Rooms overlooking Huaihai Rd may be a tad noisy at night.

☎ 6471 7000 🖳 www .jinchenhotel.com ✉ 795-809 Central Huaihai Rd Ⓜ South Shaanxi Rd 🍽 restaurant

Juying Hotel

巨鹰宾馆 (3, D2)

The rooms are slightly battered at this villa-surrounded hotel; but price, location and charm make this a serious contender. Aim to grab one of the excellent attic rooms if you can, with views over the garden.

☎ 6466 7788 ✉ 889 Julu Rd Ⓜ Changshu Rd/Jing'an Temple

Mayfair Hotel

上海巴黎春天大酒店 (2, A2)

Professional and fresh, the Mayfair combines excellent midrange value with a modern edge. The Zhongshan Park location may seem stranded, but the metro is just down the road and views extend over parkland from

the new block's slick doubles.

☎ 6240 8888 🖳 www .mayfairshanghai.com ✉ 1555 Dingxi Rd Ⓜ Zhongshan Park 🍽

Manpo Boutique Hotel

万宝大酒店 (2, A2)

With 76 smart rooms tucked away down villa and tree-lined Xinhua Rd – formerly Amherst Rd – the four-star Manpo may be pleasantly out of the action, but Hongqiao Airport is not far and the West Yan'an Rd light rail station plugs you into Shanghai's transport matrix.

☎ 6280 1000 ✉ 660 Xinhua Rd Ⓜ West Yan'an Rd light rail 🍽 restaurant, bar

Nanxinyuan Hotel

南馨园酒店 (2, C1)

Situated along charming Shanyin Rd just east of Luxun Park, this hotel has smart doubles with small, clean bathrooms and wireless Internet connection. English skills are not a forte, but room rates are low and discounts (zhékòu) add extra merit.

☎ 5696 1178 ✉ 277 Shanyin Rd Ⓜ Hongkou Stadium light rail 🍽 restaurant

Old House Inn

老时光酒店 (3, C2)

In a hopeful sign of evolution in the Shanghai hotel market, this recently opened boutique hotel has gorgeous, traditionally styled rooms and is delightfully located down an old lane.

☎ 6248 6118 🖳 www .oldhouse.cn ✉ No 16, Lane 351, Huashan Rd Ⓜ Changshu Rd/Jing'an Temple

THE PUJIANG HOTEL

First called the Richards Hotel, the Pujiang was originally located south of Suzhou Creek. In 1860, the hotel changed its name to the Astor House Hotel, before moving to its current location north of Waibaidu Bridge in 1906. Glittering bands of the rich and celebrated, sipping champagne and calculating fortunes would band here together alongside more disreputable gaggles of gamblers and scoundrels. The Kadoories, one of Shanghai's wealthiest Jewish families, acquired the hotel in the 1920s, with the guest list extending to Albert Einstein and Bertrand Russel.

Yangtze Hotel
杨子饭店 (5, F4)
Its 1930s nostalgia overlain with the tired gloss of a Chinese-managed three-star hotel, the brick and stone Art Deco lines of the Yangtze still evoke a faded charm. The rooms, most equipped with a small balcony, are very good value and the address just off the eastern edge of Renmin Park couldn't be better.
☎ 6351 7880 ▢ www.e-yangtze.com ✉ 740 Hankou Rd Ⓜ Renmin Square ✖

YMCA Hotel
青年会宾馆 (5, G5)
Built in 1929, the three-star YMCA's rather shabby dorms and doubles don't exactly hit the sweet spot, but the location – on the borders of the Old City – nicely hits the mark. The hotel operates a shuttle bus to Pudong airport.
☎ 6326 1040 ▢ www.ymcahotel.com ✉ 123 South Xizang Rd Ⓜ Renmin Square ✖ café

BUDGET

Captain Hostel
船长青年酒店 (5, J4)
All's shipshape at the able-bodied Captain, where discerning landlubbers stow themselves away with their backpacks in this lovely old building just off the Bund. Offered here are clean dorms with bunk beds, good value double rooms, bicycle hire, Internet access and a top-floor bar (Noah's).
☎ 6325 5053, 6323 5053 ▢ www.captainhostel.com.cn ✉ 37 Fuzhou Rd Ⓜ Middle Henan Rd ✖ lobby café

Hao Jiang Hotel
皓江旅馆 (5, J4)
It's in a gritty alleyway with a mere handful of rooms and communication problems can be intense, but this budget option puts you in an old brick building virtually on the Bund. Located in between Fuzhou Rd and Guangdong Rd, simple rooms come with TV, phone, shower room and air-con. Book ahead if you want the sole economy single (Y158).
☎ 3313 0878 ✉ No 5, Lane 126, Central Sichuan Rd Ⓜ Middle Henan Rd

Ming Town Hiker Youth Hostel
明堂上海旅行者青年旅馆 (5, H3)
This welcome addition to the budget hotel scene offers tidy four- and six-bed dorms with pine bunk beds, clean communal shower facilities, a bar and an excellent location – a stroll away from the Bund on the southern corner of the grand old Hengfeng Building.
☎ 6329 7889 ✉ 450 Central Jiangxi Rd Ⓜ Middle Henan Rd ✖ bar

Motel 168
莫泰连锁旅店 (3, A3)
A new chain that has covered Shanghai, with 11 branches currently, although locations are not that convenient. Standard twins are well-designed, with a clean and compact shower room. The overall effect is clean and smooth, even if the presentation is rather cheap.
☎ 5117 7777 ▢ www.motel168.com ✉ 1119 West Yan'an Rd Ⓜ Jiangsu Rd ✖ restaurant

Pujiang Hotel
浦江饭店 (5, J2)
Fabulously located north of the Bund, the recently renovated Pujiang (also called the Astor House Hotel) has it all: history, style, cast-iron banisters, grandeur, huge rooms with wooden floorboards, cavernous bathrooms, sundry original features, plus a guest list that extends to Albert Einstein. First founded in 1846, this is Shanghai's classiest back-packer mainstay and a classic address, equipped with popular dorm beds.
☎ 6324 6388 ▢ www.pujianghotel.com ✉ 15 Huangpu Rd Ⓜ Middle Henan Rd ✖ restaurant/bar

Pujiang, an old favourite.

Shanghai Hui'en Budget Motel
上海惠恩旅馆
The roar of the West Yan'an Rd flyover and the matchbox-sized singles aside, this new three-storey hotel is one of Shanghai's cheapest and you can get a room for under Y100. All rooms come with shower units and the quieter deluxe standard rooms face the rear.
☎ 5258 0666 ✉ 917 Fahuazhen Rd Ⓜ West Yan'an Rd light rail

About Shanghai

HISTORY

Shanghai may give the impression that its destiny is to lead China, but the city is actually positioned well outside the heartland of Chinese civilisation and, until recent centuries, has enjoyed marginal historic influence. Unlike China's great historic cities – Xi'an, Luoyang, Kaifeng, Datong, Nanjing or Beijing – Shanghai has never served as dynastic capital.

Set against the boundless millennia of Chinese history, Shanghai is a newcomer with a Western-looking cityscape, dating from the city's opening to Western trade in the 19th century. The occidental character of Shanghai is compounded by the scarcity of temples (outside of the Old Town), its great web of flyovers and freeways, towering high-rises and dearth of imperial monuments.

The Early Days

Neolithic settlements in the Shanghai region date back some 5900 years. In written Chinese, Shanghai is also known as 沪 (hù), a character meaning fishing traps, pointing to the settlement's development into a fishing village by the 7th century AD. By the late 17th century, a town had emerged built on fishing, trade and cotton production and a wall had been built around the Old Town area to defend against pirates.

Opium Dens

The first Opium War was snuffed out with the Treaty of Nanking in 1842, which allowed the British to prise Shanghai open by building a concession here, quickly followed by the French in 1847. By 1863, an international settlement had been added to the French and British concessions, where foreigners lived under their own jurisdiction, protected by their own soldiers in a world independent of Chinese law. The port city flourished as a prosperous manufacturing town trading in tea, silk and opium and

...he dragon in a diorama of an opium den, Shanghai Municipal History Museum

luring large numbers of Chinese migrants either seeking a living or escaping rebellion. By 1900, the city's population had mushroomed to one million. A law unto itself, Shanghai became a murky den of iniquity and vice, overseen by the Green Gang and other punitive Chinese societies. By 1930, Shanghai also boasted the tallest and grandest buildings in Asia, a racetrack, luxury hotels, glamorous restaurants, a large population of motor cars and a dazzling community of well-dressed dandies, plutocrats and socialites.

Poster celebrating mandatory relocation to the countryside to receive 're-education'.

Red Dawn

Shanghai's growing urban proletariat, workhouse squalor and rampant inequalities incubated protesting sentiments which gave birth to the Communist Party, formed here in 1921, paving the way for the inexorable rise of Mao Zedong. Chiang Kaishek's suppression of labour unrest and the massacre of workers in 1927 forced the Communists underground and they were not to return in force until 25 May 1949.

The Communist Era

With the defeat of Nationalist forces, the Communists took control of China, establishing the People's Republic of China on 1 October 1949. Under Mao Zedong, the Communists stamped out the inequalities and injustices that had plagued the city and set about renaming the city's streets and landmarks: the former racetrack was converted into People's Park and People's Square in 1952. Plunged into chaos during the Cultural Revolution (1966–76), the city stagnated until Deng Xiaoping's period of reform and opening gave the city a new lease of life after 1979. The decision to develop the Pudong area in 1990 gave Shanghai the capital and prestige it craved, turning the city into a major financial and logistics hub to rival Hong Kong.

Shanghai Today

Shanghai again finds itself on the upward arc of one of its splendid cyclical upturns. The whiff

SLEEPLESS IN SHANGHAI

A local survey detected a staggering 75% of Shanghai workers suffering from insomnia. As many as 67% of respondents claimed they slumbered for only five to six hours with a large proportion turning to medication to sleep. The brood of night owls is not just growing due to mounting work pressure, with sociologists also pointing their clipboards at the increasing variety of nocturnal entertainment options, from satellite TV, to night clubs and broadband Internet access.

Revolutionary figures ever-faithful to the little red book, antique stall at Dongtai Rd

of opium has long dispersed, but the spectre of the past still haunts Shanghai's streets: from the fading nobility of its buildings; the European streetscapes; the ballrooms and clubs; its old-timer jazz band; and a new tide of foreign money-makers. The Communist revolution is truly dead and buried when Shanghai teenagers start strolling about town in designer Che Guevara T-shirts.

It must be emphasised that Shanghai bears little resemblance to the rest of China. The Communist Party's ambition is to turn the entire country into a vast Singapore – a civic and undemocratic society where everyone does what they are told – and Shanghai is the perfect place for a dry run.

Modern Shanghai is dazzling in parts, but this can result in a blinkered sense of political reality. China remains an authoritarian state that brooks no dissent, bans freedom of speech, maintains a stranglehold on the media and easily tops the world rankings in nationwide executions.

ENVIRONMENT

Shanghai's caustic air pollution is notorious and a constant source of irritation for long-term residents in the city. Attempts at cleaning up the Shanghai environment have run into resistance from the runaway growth in the number of vehicles. A pleasant aspect is the number of well-groomed trees, but although the centre of town is clean, the suburbs rapidly get gritty and grubby as the Starbucks thin out. Shanghai's many parks serve as green lungs which sponge things up a bit, although few have substantial lawns.

Be alert to hazards especially off the main streets, from spent neon light-tubes poking out of litter bins to open manholes and welders showering the pavements with burning sparks. Side streets off the main drag are sometimes devoid of street lights at night and pavements are often crumbling and uneven. Also prepare for slippery marbled paving slabs in pedestrian areas (eg on Nanjing Rd) after the rain.

The smells on the streets can have you reeling, from traffic fumes, to sharp chemical blasts, the eye-watering aroma of *chòu dòufu* (smelly Chinese snack) pungent wafts from the city's system. Summer hatches a barrage of odours.

GOVERNMENT & POLITICS

In any other communist state, Shanghai would be seen as a brazen act of defiance, but the city's brash display of wherewithal simply has the rest of China – and even members of the Politburo – cheering and whooping.

Despite some ironclad revolutionary credentials (the Chinese Communist Party was born here in 1921), Shanghai today is a politically timid creature. As with their compatriots, the Shanghai Chinese have been hounded into silence, except when it dovetails with the government's agenda (ie anti-Japanese riots). Shanghai Chinese are moreover less cerebral and erudite than their Beijing cousins, so politics takes even more of a back seat to money-making and the flaunting of wealth.

ECONOMY

Located on the coast off the East China Sea south of the Yangzi River and situated on a major waterway (the Huangpu River), Shanghai has long been an ideal logistics base. It was this favourable location that drew wide-eyed foreign merchants and opportunists to Shanghai in the 19th century.

Not included in the first batch of Special Economic Zones (SEZ) in the 1980s, the city boarded the gravy train in 1990 when Pudong was transformed into an economic zone in its own right and Shanghai became a municipality. Since those early days, Shanghai has achieved simply staggering GDP growth, transforming the city into mainland China's financial, economic and logistics hub.

In 2005, the city was ranked 102nd in the annual US-based Mercer Human Resources Consulting urban survey. Researchers evaluate life quality indicators that include political, social and economic dimensions. The city may lag far behind Geneva and Zurich (tied first place) but lies roughly halfway up the list. More foreign banks are setting up shop in Shanghai, financial services are increasingly diverse, and both cultural and service infrastructure is developing rapidly. But as the city's booming economy shunts it up the ranks, other factors – including Shanghai's bad air-quality, congested roads and political rigidity – act as a deadweight.

When visiting Shanghai, perhaps reflect on some figures. The top 10% of Chinese people share 45% of the country's wealth, and Shanghai's citizens can be considered some of the richest in the land. Shanghai is not just the Mayfair of China in its property prices, but in the cars on its streets and the balances in its banks. With a price tag of around Y15, 000 per square metre for apartments within the first ring road, property prices have further prised open the gap between rich and poor. An estimated 80% of the city's BMWs are funded by profits from property speculation, while at the other end of the scale,

Shopping – the new opiate of the mas

immigrant workers scavenge for work (including female construction workers from other provinces). In less paradoxical circumstances, the growing disparity between the have and have-nots could well prompt revolutionary fervour. Has Shanghai come full circle?

SOCIETY & CULTURE

Shanghai has a total population approaching 15 million, and an average of 24,806 people per sq km in the downtown area.

Like Hong Kong, Shanghai can be deceptively Western. The city has long flirted with the Western perspective, but remains staunchly Chinese in its traditions and customs. Like all Chinese, the Shanghainese are particularly proud of their Chinese ancestry and concessions to Western taste are more of a badge than any partisan alliance.

The Shanghai Chinese are also physically different from Beijing folk. Beijingers are slightly taller, plumper and more solid in form than their longer-faced, skinnier and shorter Shanghai compatriots.

In many respects, the Shanghainese are similar to the Hong Kong Chinese, as both are southern Chinese from flourishing coastal port towns that historically both served as havens for refugees and flirted with Western customs and beliefs. The Shanghainese are admired by Chinese *wàidìrén* (outsiders) for their competence and envied for their successes. On the downside, they are also seen by their compatriots as being stingy, calculating, unfriendly and more than a little bit stroppy.

Shanghai has a strong regional identity, forged from its unique history, its dialect and geographical location. The city is more traditionally Chinese than Beijing, for example, in its marking of the Qingming Festival (Tomb Sweeping Day) and other events on the religious calendar. In this way, it again more closely resembles Hong Kong than Beijing.

In such a populous city, personal space is under constant pressure. You don't so much ascend the No 2 line of the metro during rush hour as ram your way in. Cyclists glance off each other on the road as relentlessly as Xiangyang Market hawkers rip down your last shreds of privacy.

... not for the claustrophobic

Dos & Don'ts

When excavating their teeth with a toothpick at mealtime, the Chinese shield the goings-on with one hand. When handing over a business card, deliver (and receive) the card Chinese-style: at the corner with the thumb and first finger of both hands, which denotes respect. You won't see Chinese pecking each other on the cheek when meeting, so try to refrain. Don't insist on paying for the dinner/bar bill if your fellow diner appears determined as this might lead to

NUMBERS

It's common knowledge that eight *(bā)* denotes luck throughout the Chinese world, while four *(sì)* is malevolent as it chimes with the word death *(sǐ)*. Dialect differences don't necessarily make things safer, as 'four' and 'death' in Cantonese are both *'seí'*. Things get complicated in Shanghai, though, as 'four' sounds like 'to lose', so it is shunned for different reasons, while six is avoided in Shanghai as it sounds like the word 'to drop' (although the number is a-OK in Beijing). In 2005, Shanghai's largest taxi firm took all taxis with number plates ending in the number four off the roads during the June high school examination period.

his/her loss of face. Face can be loosely described as 'status', 'ego' or 'self-respect', and is by no means alien to foreigners. Losing face *(diūmiànzi)* is about making someone look stupid or being forced to back down in front of others and you should take care to avoid it. If a smoker, be generous and always offer your cigarettes around. If toasted at dinner table, note who toasted you and toast them back after a few minutes.

ARTS

Shanghai has certainly blossomed artistically since the grey 1980s, but creativity – in this cosmopolitan metropolis – remains in a curious state of dwarfism and neglect. As elsewhere in China, the education system fails to nurture original-ity or a questioning creativity in children, and restraints are put on thinking outside the square. When

Putting on the finishing touches

examining the arts scene in Shanghai, it should be understood that the Chinese are also deeply conformist by nature and nurture. Pressures on Shanghai's citizens to make money and eschew the artistic path are substantial, and no more so than in Shanghai. A lack of artistic bold-ness results, although certain fields – for example architecture – display more creative invention. The increasing numbers of art galleries suggests a renaissance of sorts and an enlarged appetite for the consumption of art certainly exists. Much modern Shanghai art, however, appears unoriginal and formulaic, marked by an absence of vision. Nonethe-less, Shanghai art is often more political in content than other creative fields (eg literature), shielded by its oblique content and interpretive ambiguities.

Architecture

Shanghai has China's most diverse array of architectural styles, exceed-ing even Hong Kong or Macau. Wandering Shanghai's streets is the best way to get a taste of its eclectic architectural brew, which ranges from traditional temple architecture through Art Deco, neoclassical, socialist post-modern, post-socialist and on into uncharted territory.

By far the most elegant and charming district is the French Concession, with its French apartment blocks, villas and small cottages. If interested in Shanghai's unique architectural narrative, visit the Old China Hand Reading Room & Café (p54) which stocks a thorough selection of books on the subject.

Lilong housing in French Concession

Shanghai's urban textures are far from uniformly sleek, and brushed aluminium shop fronts regularly give way to bruised streetscapes of fractured paving slabs and grimy apartment blocks, signs suggesting both inequalities of wealth and a city fast outstripping itself. Shanghai's swish districts are in the pink, but the suburbs are grey, featureless sprawls of housing blocks and gritty streets.

The city has grown too fast and too furiously and the skyline is blighted with malformed architecture, including endless stained white-tile high-rises and the Oriental Pearl TV Tower. Shanghai also corners the market on faux classical residences. A curious hybrid spawned from the laboratory of socialism with Chinese characteristics, these overblown, concrete dwellings with classical porticos look like they've been snatched from a Hollywood film set.

Contemporary Art

Shanghai is well served with commercial and non-commercial art galleries where you can get a handle on the visual art scene. Shanghai's most famous artist is the Ningbo-born former socialist-realist artist and fashion mogul Chen Yifei (www.chenyifei.com), who died in 2005. His oil portraits of traditional musicians are abundantly counterfeited throughout China, from Kashgar to Shenzhen. For the best angle of Shanghai's contemporary art scene, a visit to 50 Moganshan Rd (p30) is mandatory.

...ading Room & Café

Literature

With its cosmopolitan past and revolutionary DNA, it comes as little surprise that Shanghai was a fertile environment for China's literati in the 1920s and 30s. Lu Xun, the father of modern Chinese literature, was born in Shaoxing in Zhejiang but he lived in Shanghai and was buried in his namesake park in Hongkou district. Other famous wordsmiths with a Shanghai connection include leftists Mao Dun and Ding Ling, the anarchist and novelist Ba Jin, and modernist writer Yu Dafu.

ARRIVAL & DEPARTURE

By far the vast majority of visitors from abroad arrive in Shanghai by air, although you can arrive by train from Hong Kong, Beijing and other major cities in China. Shanghai is also connected by ferry to ports in Japan.

Air

Shanghai has two airports, with international flights operating from the efficiently designed Pudong International Airport (opened in 1999), 30km southeast of Shanghai. International and domestic departures are adjacent to each other. Hongqiao Airport, 18km west of the Bund, has domestic connections within China. Both airports are reasonably well connected to town. Luggage storage is available at both airports.

HONGQIAO AIRPORT (2, A2)

For travellers to domestic locations, a check-in facility exists for flights after 11am at 1600 West Nanjing Rd (☎ 3214 4600), where buses run to Hongqiao Airport (Y20). Check your bags in 2½ hours before your flight departure time.

Information

General enquiries (☎ 6268 8918)
Domestic arrivals (☎ 6268 8899)
Website (www.shairport.com)
Buses (☎ 5114 6532)

Airport Access

A taxi to the centre of town will cost around Y50 (30 minutes or more). Avoid taxi sharks unless the queues are unbearable, when they can be a lifesaver (you should be able to haggle a taxi to Renmin Square down to around Y100), and prepare to queue half an hour or more for a taxi. A short-hop taxi rank, with much smaller queues, also exists for journeys close to Hongqiao Airport. Most tourist hotels operate shuttle buses to and from the airport. Airport Bus No 1 runs between Hongqiao Airport and Pudong International Airport, and a special bus leaves for Jing'an Temple (Y4; every 20 minutes).

Other useful bus lines include:

No 925 Runs to Renmin Square (one hour; Y4; every 15 minutes).
No 938 Runs to Pudong via North Caoxi Rd where you can hook up with Metro Line 1 (Shanghai Stadium Station; Y4; every 15 minutes).
No 941 Runs to Shanghai Train Station via Zhongshan Park (Y4; every 15 minutes).

PUDONG AIRPORT Information

General enquiries (☎ 6834 1000)
Domestic arrivals (☎ 3848 4500)
Website (www.shairport.com)

Airport Access

A taxi into central Shanghai will cost around Y140, taking around an hour. Shanghai's high-speed Maglev departs every 20 minutes for the eight-minute ride to Longyang Rd Station, but is far from ideal for passengers with baggage.

Pudong Airport operates seven airport bus routes. Buses depart Pudong from around 7am, leaving town earlier at 5.30am or 6am. Useful lines include:

No 1 To/from Hongqiao airport (Y22; ⊗ 7am-last flight; every 20-30 minutes)
No 2 To/from the City Air Terminal at Jing'an Temple (Y19; ⊗ 7am-last flight; every 15 minutes)
No 5 To/from Shanghai train station (Y18; ⊗ 7am-11am; every 20 minutes)
No 6 To/from West train station (Y20; ⊗ 8am-11pm; every 20-30 minutes)

Train

Train travel is an efficient and exhilarating way of seeing China. Most trains depart and arrive at **Shanghai Train Station** (Map 5, C1) in the north of town, but many southbound trains depart from the newly reconstructed **Shanghai south train station** (Map 2, A3; Guilin Rd).

There are four categories of domestic train tickets: hard seat, soft seat, hard sleeper and soft sleeper. Except for short haul trips, buy your tickets several days earlier from the railway station, a ticket booking office, a travel agent or through your hotel. The Longmen Hotel, just west of the Shanghai Train Station, is a good place to get hold of hard-sleeper tickets and tickets to Hong Kong.

Boat

Ferries (☎ 6595 6888) run every Tuesday to Osaka (Y1300-Y6500; departs 11am; 46 hours). Boats also depart every other Saturday to Kobe (Y1300-Y6500; 1pm; 48 hours), arriving the following Monday. Vessels to ports in Japan and South Korea depart from the **International Ferry Terminal** (100 Yangshupu Rd).

Bus

Bus connections link Shanghai to scores of towns and cities throughout China, although most visitors will prefer the more convenient train or plane. Useful bus stations for trips out of town include the **Hengfeng Rd bus station** (Map 5, C3), next to the Hanzhong Rd metro station and the **Xujiahui bus station** (Map 8 B1; 211 Hongqiao Rd). The **Shanghai Sightseeing Bus Centre** (Map 8, C4; under No 5 staircase, Gate 12, Shanghai Stadium, 666 Tianyaoqiao Rd) runs 10 routes to sights largely on the fringes of town.

Travel Documents
PASSPORT & VISA

All visitors to Shanghai require a visa and passport. Visas are readily available from Chinese embassies and consulates around the world. Most tourists are issued with a single-entry visa, valid for entry within three months of the date of issue (activated on the day you enter China), for a 30-day visit. Longer stays are also granted, but there is no guarantee. Visa extensions are available from the **PSB office** (☎ 6357 7925; 333 Wusong Rd; ☒ 9-11.30am & 1.30-4.30pm Mon-Sat)

Customs & Duty Free

You are allowed to import up to 400 cigarettes or the equivalent in tobacco products; 2L of alcohol; 72 rolls of still film; and 50g of gold or silver. Importation of fresh fruit is prohibited. You can legally bring in or take out only Y6000 in Chinese currency. There are no restrictions on foreign currency; however, you should declare any cash that exceeds US$5000.

GETTING AROUND

Shanghai is a large city and getting around can be both stressful and difficult. By far the fastest way to cover long distances is to take the metro. In this book, the nearest Metro station is noted after the Ⓜ icon in each listing.

Metro & Light Railway

The metro is clean, fast and the most convenient way to get around town. Trains run regularly between 5am and 11pm, with the arrival time of the next train displayed on flat TV screens. Carriages are very full during rush hour, when they frequently exceed capacity. The system extends to two lines (No 1 Line and No 2 Line), which intersect at Renmin Park/Renmin Square. There is also a light rail line which connects with the No 1 Line at Zhongshan Park and Shanghai Train Station. Single journey tickets (bought from either the machine or ticket booth) range in price from Y3 to Y6 and a combined metro, light rail, bus and taxi smart card is available. Coin-operated toilets exist on platforms at certain stations (Y1). Metro stations are identified by the red letter 'M'.

Taxi

Navigating central Shanghai by taxi is sensible, as taxis are plentiful, good value (especially for shortish hops) and simple to flag down. During rush hour, taxis can be more elusive and fares for longer rides can quickly mount up. Taxis can also be found outside tourist hotels. Empty taxis are visible by the red 'for hire' light on the dashboard of the passenger side. Ensure that the taxi driver activates the meter for all trips. The rear left hand door is often locked, so board the taxi from the right side. Flag fall is Y10 for the first 3km, and Y2 per km thereafter. From 11pm to 5am a night rate applies, when flag fall is Y13 and Y2.6 per km afterwards. Most taxi drivers are honest and usually, although not exclusively, male. Communication is tricky as few taxi drivers speak English, so have the name of your destination written in Chinese. Fares can be electronically deducted from the combined metro and bus card (*shuākǎ*). There is no need to tip. Ask for a printed receipt (*fāpiào*) as the driver's ID number will appear on it along with the taxi company's phone number, in the event that you leave something in the taxi. Often the only seat belts are in the front passenger seat. Shanghai's main taxi companies are **Dazhong** (☎ 6318 5666), **Qiangsheng** (☎ 6258 0000) and **Jinjiang** (☎ 6275 8800).

Bicycle

With around nine million bicycles in Shanghai, the era of the bike is far from running out of pedal power. Cycling remains an excellent, low-tech way to navigate the centre town. Note, however, that bicycles are now banned from several major roads – 'to improve traffic conditions' – so cyclists are forced to mount the pavements instead.

Bus

While the bus network in Shanghai is extensive and tickets are cheap (Y1 to Y2), the cut and thrust of rush hour rapidly depletes enthusiasm. Most visitors to Shanghai take either the metro or taxis.

Maglev

The sleek German-designed Maglev (p26) is more a futuristic novelty than a practical mode of transport for travellers laden with heavy bags. Despite sleek lines, colossal speeds (430 km/h) and a swift journey time of just eight minutes, the Maglev (economy single/return

Y50/80, Y40 with air ticket; from 8.20am to 5.40pm; every 20 minutes) only connects Pudong International Airport with Longyang Rd station, still in Pudong. Nonetheless, a trip on the train is thrilling and a return ticket to the airport is a fun outing.

Car & Motorcycle

Tourists are not permitted to hire cars in Shanghai. This is not such a huge sacrifice, as Shanghai's roads are truly lethal. To drive in Shanghai, you will need a Chinese driving licence and a residency permit, which renders the Avis office at Pudong airport useless for foreign arrivals.

PRACTICALITIES
Business Hours

Banks, offices and government departments are usually open Monday to Friday from 9am to noon and about 2pm to 4.30pm. Post offices are open daily 8.30am to 6pm and sometimes later (local post offices close at weekends). Most museums are open at weekends (they usually stop selling tickets 30 minutes before closing) and some close on Mondays. Most shops and department stores stay open till around 10pm.

Climate & When to Go

The best time to visit Shanghai is April to mid-May, when the magnolias are in blossom and the city is warming up, although autumn (late September to mid-November) is also pleasant and several interesting arts festivals are held. Temperatures in April can still top 30°C (86°F), however, bringing with it Huangmei Tian (literally 'Yellow Plum Days') – the name given to the warm, steamy weather of April and

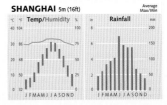

SHANGHAI 5m (16ft)

May – and locals start wandering the streets in pyjamas. December and January are dismal, overcast and unpleasantly cold. The temperature can creep below freezing, although it seldom snows. Summer ushers in the peak travel season but the sweltering temperatures of July and August – as high as 40°C (104°F) – are best avoided. Note that winter and summer are also the peak pollution seasons.

Disabled Travellers

While Shanghai has superior facilities for the disabled traveller compared to other cities in China, the city is still inadequately equipped to deal with those in wheelchairs. Bicycles and scooters take to the uneven pavements, kerbs are high and escalators in the metro only go up. In this book, the ♿ symbol has been awarded only to places with ramps and lifts/elevators, and where wheelchairs can be manoeuvred.

Electricity

Voltage 220V
Frequency 50Hz
Cycle AC
Plugs: Most plugs will take four designs: three-pronged angled pins, three-pronged round pins, two flat pins and two narrow round pins.

Consulates

Canada (Map 5, B5; ☎ 6279 8400; www.shanghai.gc.ca; Suite 604, Shanghai Centre, 1376 West Nanjing Rd ⏰ 8.30am-5pm Mon-Fri; visa section 8.45am-11am Mon-Thu for applications & 1.30pm-4pm for passport pickup)
UK (Map 5, B5; ☎ 6279 7650; www .uk.cn/bj/index.asp?city=4; Suite 301, Shanghai Centre, 1376 West Nanjing Rd; ⏰ 8.30am-12.30pm & 1.30-3.30pm Mon-Fri, to 5pm Mon-Thu)
USA (Map 3, C4; ☎ 6433 6880; www .usembassy-china.org.cn/shanghai; 1469 Central Huaihai Rd; ⏰ 8am-11.30am & 1.30-3.30pm, closed Tue afternoon and all day Sat & Sun)

Emergencies

Apart from crossing the road, Shanghai is generally a very safe place to visit and walking around at night presents few hazards.
Ambulance (☎ 120)
Fire (☎ 119)
Police (☎ 110)

Fitness

Shanghai abounds in gyms and fitness centres. If you've had one too many *xiǎolóngbāo* (steamed dumpling), consider a spell at **Total Fit** (Map 5, D5; ☎ 6255 3535; 5th & 6th fl, 819 West Nanjing Rd). This vast place has the full range of equipment, facilities (including a boxing ring) and courses – from aerobics, yoga, through to Thai boxing and beyond.

Gay & Lesbian Travellers

The law is quite ambiguous on the issue of homosexuality and gays and lesbians generally adopt a low profile in Shanghai. For information on the latest gay and lesbian venues in Shanghai, visit the **Utopia Website** (www.utopia-asia.com/chinshan .htm). See the entertainment chapter for listings of gay and lesbian bars in town.

Health
IMMUNISATIONS

No vaccination requirements exist, except for proof of a yellow fever vaccination if arriving from an infected area. It's recommended though that you ensure your tetanus, diphtheria and polio vaccinations are up to date. Vaccinations against hepatitis A and B, Japanese encephalitis and typhoid are also worth considering.

PRECAUTIONS

Visitors with asthma or other allergies may react badly to the air quality, which is dreadful. Stick to bottled mineral water or boiled water and avoid drinking tap water. Traveller's diarrhoea is common among visitors to China – make sure you thoroughly wash fruit and vegetables. Influenza during the winter months is a further hazard, while the high humidity and temperatures of summer can be draining. The latest news on SARS (Severe Acute Respiratory Syndrome) and other health-related information can be found online at www.who.int/countries/en/.

MEDICAL SERVICES

Travel insurance is advisable to cover any medical treatment you may need while in Shanghai. Treatment at Chinese hospitals is not expensive and is of a reasonably high quality. Standards of medical care at Western clinics are generally quite high, but they are expensive. Hospitals with 24-hour accident and emergency departments include:

Huashan Hospital (Map 3, H2; ☎ 6248 9999, ext 2531; 12 Central Wulumuqi Rd) Hospital treatment and out-patient consultations are available at the 15th-fl foreigners' clinic (☘ 8am-5pm Mon-Fri; 24-hr emergency treatment).

Shanghai United Family Hospital (Map 2, A2; ☎ 5133 1900; emergency hotline ☎ 5133 1999; www.unitedfamilyhospitals.com; 1139 Xianxia Rd, Changning district)

DENTAL SERVICES

If you chip a tooth or require emergency treatment, head to:

Arrail Dental (Map 3, H1: ☎ 5396 6538; www.arrail-dental.com; Unit 204, Lippo Plaza, 222 Central Huaihai Rd; Ⓜ South Huangpi Rd)

PHARMACIES

Shanghai pharmacies are abundant and are signalled by a green cross (often illuminated). Usually open until around 8pm, pharmacies stock both Chinese and Western medicine. Take the generic name of any prescriptions you may need and not just the brand name. Many drugs are available without prescription.

Holidays

New Year's Day 1 January.
Chinese New Year (Spring Festival) A week-long holiday.
International Labour Day 1 May. A week-long break.
National Day 1 October. A week-long break.

Information & Organisations

If you want to locate or contact a tourist, entertainment, shopping or business venue and have a mobile phone, then text message the name of the venue to the wireless search engine **GuanXi** (☎ 885074). The name, address and directions, plus telephone number will be immediately returned to you by SMS (Y1-Y2 per enquiry). The information can also be relayed in Chinese if your phone has the settings.

Internet

Shanghai is the country's most wired city and Internet cafés are widespread. Note however that the Internet is rigorously policed by an Internet Gestapo some 30,000 strong, blocking tens of thousands of (often innocuous) websites. If interested in websites blocked by the authorities, take a look at the exhaustively researched www.cyber.law.harvard.edu/filtering/china/. Wireless connections are available at numerous hotels and bars/restaurants (eg Big Bamboo).

INTERNET CAFÉS

When looking for an Internet café, look for the following characters 网吧 *(wǎngbā)*. Some are open 24 hours, many of which are full of kids playing online games. Prices start at around Y2 per hour. Some cafés, such as Boonna Café allow guests to get online free. Free Internet (single terminal, 30-minute use) is also available at **Shanghai Information Centre for International Visitors** (Map 3, H2; ☎ 6384 9366; No 2, Alley 123, Xingye Rd, Xintiandi) and **Eastday B@r** (Map 3, F2; 24 Ruijin No 2 Rd; Y3 per hour; ☘ 8am-2am). The **Shanghai Library** (Map

3, C4; ☎ 6445 5555; 1555 Central Huaihai Rd; Y4 per hour; 🕙 8.30am-8.30pm) has a useful and popular Internet café.

USEFUL WEBSITES

The Lonely Planet website (www.lonely planet.com) offers a speedy link to many of Shanghai's websites.

Cityweekend (www.cityweekend.com.cn) Excellent on-line information on entertainment in Shanghai.

Shanghai Expat (http://shanghai.asiaxpat .com/) Very useful expat service website with forum, classifieds, member blogs etc.

Tales of Old China (www.talesofoldchina .com) Excellent source of historical information on Shanghai.

Zanhe (www.zanhe.com) Fascinating website dedicated to promoting the Shanghainese dialect.

Asia Expat Shanghai (www.shanghai .asiaxpat.com/directory.htm) Reams of useful information.

Metric System

The metric system is used in Shanghai. When buying fruit and vegetables from street vendors, you are likely to encounter the Chinese system: *liǎng* and *jīn*. One *jīn* is 0.6kg (1.32lb) and one *liǎng* is 37.5g (1.32oz), with 16 *liǎng* to the *jīn*.

Money
ATMS

Shanghai's ATMs increasingly accept foreign credit and debit cards and are widespread at most large department stores, malls and top-end and deluxe hotels. ATMs with international access can also be found at some tourist sights, such as the ground floor of the Shanghai Museum. HSBC also has several branches in town with 24-hour ATMs.

CREDIT CARDS

You will see logos for major international credit cards all over town, but they are generally only accepted at tourist hotels, restaur-

ants and shops that see foreign customers. The Chinese are no fans of living on credit; consequently the credit card industry in China is small. Credit card cash advances can be made at Bank of China branches (for a 4% commission). The following are emergency contact numbers in case you lose your card:

American Express (☎ 6279 8082; 9am-noon & 1-5.30pm) Out of business hours call the 24-hour refund line in Hong Kong (☎ 852 2811 6122).

MasterCard (1080 0110 7309)

Visa (108 0010 2911)

CURRENCY

The Chinese currency is known as Renminbi (RMB). The basic unit is the yuán (Y), known in spoken Chinese as *kuài*. One yuán is divided into 10 *jiǎo* (*máo* in spoken Chinese), itself divided into the rarely seen fen. Paper notes are issued in denominations of one, two, five, 10, 20, 50 and 100 yuán; and one, two and five *jiǎo*. Coins appear in denominations of one yuán; and one, two and five *jiǎo*. Large denomination notes are often checked for their authenticity at shops and supermarkets.

MONEYCHANGERS

You can change foreign currency and travellers cheques at money changing counters at most hotels, large banks and at some department stores (take your passport). Exchange rates in China are uniform, so there's no need to shop around. Black-market money changers are not worth the hassle. RMB is difficult to change abroad so hang onto your exchange receipts so that you can change your RMB back into your home currency when leaving China.

TRAVELLERS CHEQUES

Travellers cheques not only provide security, but they also offer a marginally better exchange rate than cash. Cheques from most of the world's leading banks and issuing agencies are now accepted in China, but try to use Thomas Cook, American Express or Citibank.

Newspapers & Magazines

The *Shanghai Daily* (Y1; Monday to Saturday, it's not quite a daily) is a far better read than the anaemic *China Daily*, which is not only dry as dust but in the mornings is often a day out of date. The *Shanghai Daily* still answers to the propaganda department, but its international coverage – albeit largely from wires – is thorough and *Scope*, the cultural section, has some absorbing articles on Shanghai culture.

Foreign magazines and newspapers, including the *International Herald Tribune*, *Financial Times*, *Newsweek*, *Asian Wall Street Journal*, *Time* and *Economist* are available in top-end hotels. Shanghai also has several English-language culture and lifestyle magazines aimed at visitors and expats. These include *City Weekend*, *8 Days*, *That's Shanghai* and *Shanghai Scene*, available free from expat bars, restaurants, tourist hotels and some art galleries.

For a country expected to shape the 21st century, the media outlook is grim. The world's most professional and impartial news organisation – the BBC – has its marvellous Chinese language news website continuously blocked and even more shamefully, www.news.bbc.co.uk is often inaccessible.

Photography & Video

Colour print film (Kodak, Fuji) is widely available but is largely 100 ISO. Slide film is not that hard to find and film processing is everywhere (Kodak).

China subscribes to the PAL broadcasting standard, the same as Australia, New Zealand, the UK and most of Europe.

Post

Post offices, fronted in green, are widespread, although you can also use the post offices in tourist hotels and international business towers for mailing letters and small packages.

Shanghai's international post office (Map 5, H2) is located in a historic British building at the corner of North Sichuan Rd and North Suzhou Rd. The international mail counters are open daily from 7am to 7pm, and until 10pm in the upstairs room. Mailboxes on the street are coloured green.

The domestic postal service is efficient. Letters take about a week to reach most overseas destinations and Express Mail Service cuts this down to three or four days. Courier companies can take as little as two days.

POSTAL RATES

Registered mail costs extra, but cheaper postal rates are available for printed matter, small packets, parcels, bulk mailings and so on.

An airmail letter costs Y5.40 to Y6.40 for around 20g everywhere except Hong Kong, Macau and Taiwan (Y2.50). A postcard costs Y4.20 (Y1.5 to Hong Kong). A domestic letter/postcard costs Y0.80/Y0.30.

Radio

The BBC World Service can be picked up on 17760, 15278, 21660, 12010 and 9740 kHz. Voice of America (VOA) is often a little clearer at 17820, 15425, 21840, 15250, 9760, 5880 and 6125 kHz. You can find tuning information for the BBC on the web at www.bbc.co.uk/worldservice/tuning/, for Radio Australia at www.abc.net.au/ra/, and for VOA at www.voa.gov/. Crystal clear programmes from the BBC World Service can be heard on-line: follow the links on www.bbc.co.uk/worldservice/.

Telephone

Local calls from coin-operated payphones cost Y1 (or use an IC card) Many small hole-in-the-wall shops have phones you can use for local calls.

PHONE CARDS

IC cards can be useful for local calls made from public payphones; for overseas and long distance calls, IP cards offer the cheapest rates and can be used on your hotel phone. Both cards are available from newspaper kiosks, convenience stores and post offices.

MOBILE PHONES

For most mobile phones, you can buy a pay-as-you-go card to slot into your phone from both China Mobile and China Unicom, which both operate on the GSM system.

COUNTRY & CITY CODES

Drop the first '0' from the city code if calling from outside China

People's Republic of China (☎ 86)
Shanghai (☎ 021)
Beijing (☎ 010)

USEFUL PHONE NUMBERS

Local Directory Enquiries (☎ 114)
International Directory Enquiry (☎ 116)
International Operator (☎ 95115)
Ambulance (☎ 120)
Police (☎ 110)
Weather (☎ 121)

Television

CCTV9 is the English language channel of China Central TV (CCTV). Content is carefully manipulated and news items selected to portray China in the best possible light. CCTV4 also has English-language news programmes on weekdays at 7pm and 11pm, and at noon on the weekend. Satellite TV is simple to arrange for residents (around 90% of satellite TV for individual users in Shanghai is pirated, costing around Y1600 for a one-off installation with no subsequent charge). Otherwise, midrange and top-end hotels provide CNN, BBC News 24, ESPN, HBO and other channels.

Time

Shanghai time is eight hours ahead of GMT/UTC. There is no daylight-saving time.

Tipping

Tipping is generally not expected (eg in taxis) although a service charge is often built into the bill at restaurants.

Toilets

Public toilets (both squat and sitting) are ubiquitous; carry tissues around with you as some loos do not come equipped with toilet paper. Hotels and fast-food chains generally have clean toilets. Some metro stations are equipped with platform coin-operated toilets.

Tourist Information

Branches of the Tourist Information & Service Centres are dotted hopefully around town. Frequently manned by bovine staff, they are not much use unless you wish to join a tour. Standards of English also vary greatly from branch to branch. Locations include:

Tourist Information & Service Centre (☎ 5386 1882, 5382 7330; 127 South Chengdu Rd; 3, H2)
Tourist Information & Service Centre (☎ 6355 5032; 149 Jiujiaochang Rd; 4, B1)

The **Tourist Hotline** (☎ 6253 4058; ☺ 10am-9pm) has quite a useful English-language service.

Women Travellers

Female travellers will encounter few problems in Shanghai as Chinese men are generally neither macho nor disrespectful to women. Shanghai is a very cosmopolitan city, so women can largely wear what they like. Tampons can be bought everywhere, although it is advisable for you to bring your own contraceptive pills.

LANGUAGE

The official language of the People's Republic of China is *Putonghua* (Mandarin), based on the Beijing dialect. Mandarin is spoken everywhere in Shanghai, but the local dialect is *Shanghaihua* (p32), which belongs to the *Wu* dialect. English is of limited use, so it is advisable to pack a phrasebook such as Lonely Planet's Mandarin Phrasebook.

Index

See also separate indexes for Eating (p93), Sleeping (p93), Entertainment (p93), Shopping (p94) and Sights with map references (p94).

SHOPPING

SIGHTS

FEATURES

Quanjude	*Eating*
Tang Hui	*Entertainment*
Eddy's Bar	*Drinking*
Bonomi Café	*Café*
Longhua Temple & Pagoda	*Highlights*
Silk King	*Shopping*
Art Scene China	*Sights/Activities*
Grand Hyatt	*Sleeping*

AREAS

	Beach, Desert
	Building
	Land
	Mall
	Other Area
	Park/Cemetery
	Sports
	Urban

HYDROGRAPHY

	River, Creek
	Intermittent River
	Canal
	Swamp
	Water

BOUNDARIES

	State, Provincial
	Regional, Suburb
	Ancient Wall

ROUTES

	Tollway
	Freeway
	Primary Road
	Secondary Road
	Tertiary Road
	Lane
	Under Construction
	One-Way Street
	Unsealed Road
	Mall/Steps
	Tunnel
	Walking Path
	Walking Trail/Track
	Pedestrian Overpass
	Walking Tour

TRANSPORT

	Airport, Airfield
	Bus Route
	Cycling, Bicycle Path
	Ferry
	General Transport
	Metro
	Monorail
	Rail
	Taxi Rank
	Tram

SYMBOLS

	Bank, ATM
	Buddhist
	Castle, Fortress
	Christian
	Diving, Snorkeling
	Embassy, Consulate
	Hospital, Clinic
	Information
	Internet Access
	Islamic
	Jewish
	Lighthouse
	Lookout
	Monument
	Mountain, Volcano
	National Park
	Parking Area
	Petrol Station
	Picnic Area
	Point of Interest
	Police Station
	Post Office
	Ruin
	Telephone
	Toilets
	Zoo, Bird Sanctuary
	Waterfall